The Luscombes

Stanley G. Thomas

The
Flying Classics
SERIES

TAB AERO

Blue Ridge Summit, PA 17294-0850

FIRST EDITION
FIRST PRINTING

© 1991 by **TAB/AERO Books**, an imprint of TAB Books.
TAB Books is a division of McGraw-Hill, Inc.

Library of Congress Cataloging-in-Publication Data

Thomas, Stanley G.
    The Luscombes / by Stanley G. Thomas.
      p.   cm.
    Includes bibliographical references and index.
    ISBN 0-8306-3618-8
    1. Luscombe airplanes—History. I. Title.
  TL686.L87T46 1991
  338.7'629133'340973—dc20   91-17846
                            CIP

TAB Books offers software for sale. For information and a catalog, please contact TAB Software Department, Blue Ridge Summit, PA 17294-0850.

Acquisitions Editor: Jeff Worsinger
Book Editor: Steve Mesner
Production: Katherine G. Brown
Series Design: Jaclyn J. Boone

Contents

9 ▶ Buying and flying the Silvaire   119

Organizations   126

About the author   127

Index   128

Foreword

When Stan Thomas asked us to write a foreword for his new book on Luscombes, he wanted us to try to explain how Don Luscombe had such long-lasting effect on so many people.

For the past decade or so, we have been attending the Annual Luscombe Airplane Fly-Ins held by the Continental Luscombe Association at Columbia, CA. As many as 100 or more restored Luscombes appear here, and the owners and their families have a wonderful reunion! I still feel a little guilty when we fly in with our shiny silver, all-original Model 35 Beechcraft Bonanza and jokingly call it our "inverted Luscombe." This year (1989) marked our 50th wedding anniversary, the anniversary of our elopement in a Luscombe airplane. The "old-timer" alumni group who were with Don Luscombe when he first started producing airplanes (along with the original staff and workers that I knew in West Trenton, NJ, from 1935 to 1939) were there to celebrate and reminisce for hours! Most of them have been coming to these Luscombe Fly-Ins from all over the country, pilgrimages in tribute to Don Luscombe, his famous little airplanes and his "family" of supporters.

When I went to work for this little new airplane company at the local airport in West Trenton, I was just 18 years old and had been out of high school about a year. This was during the Great Depression and jobs were scarce. Brownee Luscombe had been Don's secretary for years and took care of all the detail work. I found I practically had to learn a new language—I had never heard the words and didn't know how to spell things such as fuselage, aileron, and so forth. I had to be "educated" into aviation and was the butt of many jokes, such as, "Now, where did you put that bucket of prop wash?" I was fascinated with everyone and everything—enthusiastic, starry-eyed, and completely captivated with the exciting world of flying. I came from a big, Catholic, Italian family and had never been away from home so the Luscombe people became my "wonderful new family." I would rave on and on about them at home so much that my brothers and sisters would scream in protest and cover their ears.

Everyone was devoted to Don Luscombe. They would do anything for him and worked long hours, night and day, and sometimes even without pay for weeks! They believed in him completely and were dedicated to him and to the development of the fantastic planes he designed and hoped to produce. Don was a "charmer," a super salesman, a terrific promoter, and a "con man" of many talents. His wife adored him but she didn't trust him out of her sight; whenever we worked late, she would stay close. She often told me that if she ever caught him "fooling around with another woman," she would "shoot them both!"

I occasionally spent the night at the Luscombes' house when we had lots of extra work to get out, and I learned how "wild and sophisticated" they were. They had their own darkroom in their house and Don was almost a professional photographer. He printed all kinds of photos for the company and for their own amusement. That's where I first saw nude photos and Brownee enjoyed giving me "shocking" information that was a real sex education for me. I remember rushing home to whisper the details to my sisters and brothers so they "benefitted" too!

I didn't realize that Don Luscombe was a "womanizer" and eventually this was his undoing, as well as the "drinking" he did. The dissipation was beginning to be apparent even then, but he had the ability to flatter and compliment so expertly that he made you feel special and you would forgive him anything! Evidently most of his staff knew him well, and I didn't realize at the time that they were protecting and "looking out for" me when they would hang around the office during those late hours. I remember how disillusioned I was when I heard him giving the same line to another female worker and how completely she believed him too.

When word got around that Don Luscombe was going to leave the company he worked so hard, so long, and so desperately to develop, we were all shocked and saddened. I don't know whether he was a poor manager or whether the company was costing much more than he ever dreamed it would. It seemed as if he was constantly bringing in more investors and thinking out more schemes to raise money. He wrote glowing letters; his vocabulary was truly remarkable and I used to spend hours looking up the spelling of words in the dictionary! He seemed so brilliant and inventive that it just didn't seem possible he would ever give up.

I remember he had a birthday before he left the company and I wrote a verse for him. He was quite touched by the sentiment, but told me not to be so serious, that he would soon come up with new ideas and new plans. I'd like to include the verse here, as it showed how his "family of workers" felt about him.

To Don A. Luscombe—On his birthday—1939

It's difficult for me to say
The things I wish for you today.
Like the Great Shepherd and his Flock,
You helped us over each "high rock,"
And when we reached the "meadow land,"
You took away your guiding hand.
Your strength was gone, your work was done,
But, oh, "D.A.," our love you've won!
And we all know, though on we strive
Because of you we are "alive!"

I left the company on July 12, 1939, when I eloped with Jerry Coigny in our "Honeymoon Special" Luscombe airplane. Many of the original staff left that year also. It was so different working for the new president of the company, John Torrens. He was a businessman—so different from Don Luscombe—and all the magic was gone! I found out years later that Don became very bitter and never got over the loss of his company. His drinking and "womanizing" got him into all kinds of trouble and turned his friends away. Brownee eventually divorced him. Years later, when Don became very ill, he spent his last years with his first wife, Eleanor. Of course I never knew him in later years; all I remember of him were the years 1935 to 1939, when he and his airplane changed the direction of my life and brought me Jerry Coigny, who also loved the Luscombe airplane. Jerry spent years spreading Don Luscombe's fame whenever and wherever we flew to sell and demonstrate the airplane.

Lucy (Rago) Coigny
Miramonte, CA

My first experience with a Luscombe-inspired product was in 1934. My first flying lesson was in a snappy little side-by-side cabin monoplane. It was called a Velie Monocoupe. It was several years later that I learned Don Luscombe was responsible for the development of the Monocoupe. This and many of Don's other accomplishments are told in this book by Stan Thomas.

In 1937, while working for Douglas Aircraft Co. repairing DC-3s at the United Air Lines repair base in Cheyenne, WY, I saw an advertisement in *Western Flying* magazine. The prototype Luscombe 50 was pictured. I had to have one! I traded in my 40-hp T-Craft as a down payment.

Douglas Aircraft was grooming me for a lead job with a promising future, but I was counting the months waiting for my "dream ship." Carlton Darneal came by where I was working on DC-2s at about 3:00 P.M. one day in July 1938 and told me to be ready the next morning to fly to Trenton, NJ, in a Waco cabin plane belonging to Tom Warner, Luscombe Distributor for the western states.

When I got to the factory, I found I had to wait a few weeks for my airplane, and Don Luscombe put me to work driving rivets in my own airplane! I asked Don's secretary, Lucy Rago, to be my first passenger, and that was the start of the romance that will always be a part of the Luscombe story.

Most of the employees of Luscombe wanted to fly the new 50, so I made enough money for the first monthly payment on NC-2591. I was told that barnstorming was a thing of the past but it was easy to prove that wasn't true with such an eye-pleasing craft.

Several books are being prepared about Luscombes, but in my opinion, Mr. Thomas's book fills in many interesting details in a story too rich to be told by only one or two authors in one or two books, from just one or two points of view! I am sure you will thoroughly enjoy this book, as I have.

Jerry Coigny
Miramonte, CA

Acknowledgments

A host of people too numerous to mention have helped me to tell the Luscombe story. But there are many others whose contributions have been of such value that they must be recognized individually.

Dedicated fans of the Luscombe airplanes will immediately recognize the first group of names. These are the "Luscombe Alumni," that diverse group of people who were at one time employed building Luscombe airplanes. The senior member is Jerome Lederer, who went to work for Don Luscombe in 1927 at the Central States Aero company in Bettendorf, IA. He developed the technical data required to certify the Model 22 Monocoupe. The other Alumni who contributed to my research are: Chuck Burgess, Jerry and Lucy Coigny, Marty Eisenmann, Keith Funk, Frank Johnson, Howard Jong, Fritz King, Ora May "Brownee" Luscombe, Paul McCormick, Ben Melcher, Merle Mueller, Eugene Norris, Ignatius Sargent, and Bill Shepard.

Many Luscombe buffs gave me considerable assistance as well. In this group are numbered Dorothy Baker, John Bergeson, Loren Bump, Kathy Coghill, Doug Combs, Steve and Jan Dyer, Dale Folkerts, Dwayne Green, Jim Harvey, William T. Larkins, Moody Larsen, Jack Norris, Eric Presten, Ron Price, John Swick, Walt Trelenberg, John Underwood, Gar Williams, and Jim Zazas.

I am indebted to them all.

Introduction

The year 1946, when I learned to fly, was a magical one for general aviation. Tens of thousands of new airplanes poured out of the factories and soared aloft into America's skies. The flood of new aircraft penetrated every corner of the United States, including the thinly populated farm country of north-central Idaho where I grew up. Glistening Cessna 140s, Ercoupes, Globe Swifts, Cub-yellow J-3s, Luscombe Silvaires, Navions, Stinson Voyagers, and Taylorcraft BC-12Ds appeared at the local airports in increasing numbers.

In those halcyon days a high school youth with a steady part-time job could afford to learn to fly (I earned my pilot's license before I received my high school diploma). The price of the new airplanes was reasonable. The new flying clubs that sprang up could afford them and a young man with a new private license could easily aspire to own one. Not many years after I graduated from college, I did become an owner when I purchased a second-hand Cessna 140, a postwar design. It bore a striking resemblance to the Luscombe Model 8—which, I learned, was a *prewar* design!

As time went on, I learned a little more about the Luscombe's background. I learned the name of Don Luscombe. And I picked up scattered fragments of information (partly true? mostly true?) about Don Luscombe's airplanes and the other designs that they inspired. For example, late one July afternoon at Oshkosh I strolled through the Classic Airplanes exhibition area with the co-owner of a clipped-wing Monocoupe. She pointed to a Howard DGA and described how Bennie Howard was so impressed after a ride in the speedy Monocoupe that he swore he was going to have a plane just like it, only bigger. We walked past a Luscombe Model 8. She explained that Don Luscombe had wanted to build an airplane as popular as his Monocoupe had been, except built of metal.

The woman's comments were news to me, because I had never read a book about Don Luscombe's airplanes. I had read books that told the story of Travel Airs and of Cessnas and of Beeches, but I had never run across a book about the Luscombes. Then one day I received the opportunity to *write* the book I would like to have read. I was given the chance to offer a book proposal on *The Luscombes* for the "Flying Classics" series that TAB Books was planning. I responded immediately.

Most of the Luscombes were built after World War II, but the Model 8 had first flown *before* the war. In fact, the Model 8 had first flown more than half a century ago. Nevertheless, I was convinced that it would still be possible to find and talk with people who had participated in the events of those bygone years.

Once upon a time I had written a history of the settlement of my hometown. At that time I was able to obtain the recollections of quite a number of old-timers, some of whom were adults before the turn of the century and had homesteaded on the prairie. Two of them had come west on the Oregon Trail! Later, I began interviewing pioneers in aviation technology. Some of them, such as Carl Crane, Jimmy Doolittle, Matty Laird, Dean Smith, C. G. Taylor, and Fred Weick, had begun their careers in the early 1920s or even before. So it was an article of faith with me that, with diligence, I would be able to locate a number of old-timers who had built and flown and sold Luscombe airplanes in the 1930s. Thus, I would be able to add a personal touch to a story about Don Luscombe's airplanes. That I could discover eyewitnesses certainly proved to be true, as the Acknowledgments page richly attests.

The story of Don Luscombe's airplanes begins with the Monocoupe that predated Charles Lindbergh's remarkable New York to Paris flight in May 1927. The last factory-produced Luscombe was rolled out of the Silvaire Aircraft Company's Fort Collins, CO, facility many years ago. But enthusiastic and dedicated Luscombe owners, pilots, and "Alumni" still abound. The story is not over. This book embraces it all.

1

The Monocoupe is born

On a Saturday night late in May 1927, a young air mail pilot, Charles A. Lindbergh, landed at Le Bourget airfield, successfully completing a non-stop transAtlantic flight from New York to Paris. The event sparked an explosion of interest in aviation throughout America. The previous month, on April 1, there occurred the maiden flight of an airplane that was to capitalize on that interest. The airplane—to become known as the Monocoupe—would make an indelible mark on the history of light aircraft. The name of the airplane's creator, Don Luscombe, would become a legend in that history.

Don Luscombe studied merchandising at the University of Iowa, but he left college during World War I. He went overseas and drove ambulances for the French Army and later for the American Expeditionary Forces. Luscombe first became interested in flying while serving in the Paris sector. During his free time, he would trade American cigarettes for rides with French crews ferrying planes from field to field. Sometimes they would let him take the controls for a while.

After the war, Luscombe opened a small advertising agency in Davenport, IA. On the outskirts of nearby Bettendorf was a little airfield maintained by Frank Wallace, the personnel manager of the Bettendorf Car Company. Luscombe's interest in flying was renewed and he re-entered the flying community. In Wallace's shed was a war-surplus Curtiss Jenny that had never been uncrated. Eventually Luscombe took up flying seriously and bought the airplane for $850.

Opposite: Designer Clayton Folkerts and prototype model 90. Sportplane hanging from rafters is Folkerts' geodetic 20-hp single-seater. Dale Folkerts

Don Luscombe seated in the cockpit of his Curtiss JN-4. Luscombe set out to create a personal plane that would be everything that the Jenny was not.

The Jenny didn't suit Luscombe at all. It was incredibly clumsy on the ground, and slow and uncomfortable in flight. The Jenny's open cockpits were cold and drafty, so the pilot and passenger had to suit up in flying togs to go flying. Preflight and postflight chores (topping the radiator with fresh water, lubricating the rocker arms, and the like) were very time-consuming. On the ground the Jenny required the services of three men and a boy. It had no brakes and was so unwieldy that most ground maneuvers required that wing walkers help by grabbing the lower wingtips. Moving the airplane into or out of a hangar was a real effort. It weighed nearly 1600 pounds with dry tanks, spanned more than 43 feet, and was tailheavy to boot.

The Jenny did not redeem itself in flight. With a power loading of 21 pounds per horsepower the climb rate was excruciatingly slow. Its 60 mph cruise speed was little better.

Don Luscombe sold his JN-4 and bought an OX-5 powered Swallow, which was an improvement—but not much.

There had to be a better way.

Luscombe began to conceive of his "dream airplane" for the sportsman pilot. He envisioned a compact two-seater monoplane with an enclosed cabin that he could manage by himself and fly in comfort while dressed in business clothes.

Luscombe began to create his dream airplane. He reasoned that the airplane could be made much smaller and lighter if pilot and passenger were seated side by side. Additional weight could be saved if a strut-braced monoplane configuration were used instead of the draggy biplane construction that was then so common. Not only could a smaller airplane use a smaller, lighter engine, but additional gains could be realized by using one of the lightweight air-cooled engines that were beginning to appear on the market. Of course the design would have an enclosed cabin. Luscombe preferred business suits to flying togs and asserted that his passenger ought to ride along in comfort in a party dress or pajamas.

These ideas were rather advanced in 1926. They were considered heretical by many pilots, who firmly believed that a flier had to "feel the wind in his face" to control his aircraft.

The real inspiration behind Luscombe's design came from Belgium. Messrs. Demonty and Poncelet of SABCA had produced the "Limousine" late in 1924. The unusual (for that period) design was a strut-braced monoplane (featuring folding wings) with a fully enclosed cabin, side-by-side seating, and dual controls. Aft of the cabin, the distinctive-looking fuselage decreased quite rapidly in cross-section. The Demonty-Poncelet boasted a respectable 78 mph top speed with its 45-hp Anzani engine. Luscombe was impressed. He wrote for a technical report and filed it away for future reference.

Next, Don began to flesh out his idea with a cabin mockup. He fashioned this crude mockup out of lath and cardboard using old oil cans for seats. He used his own measurements and tailored the cockpit accordingly.

Don Luscombe's thoughts went beyond creating a homebuilt for his own enjoyment. His well-honed merchandising instincts told him that there was a market for his airplane. The smooth-talking Luscombe obtained the financial help he needed from the Davenport Flying Club. This organization, of which Luscombe was now a director, consisted mainly of nonflying businessmen who were interested in developing commercial aviation within the community. The members tossed about $5,000 into the pot and formed the Central States Aero Company in October 1926.

But Don was neither a designer nor a builder. Now he needed help from someone who possessed both these skills. His answer came in the person of a young Iowa farmer who farmed in the summer months and experimented with airplanes in the winter.

Clayton Folkerts

Clayton Folkerts and his brother Ed had first been exposed to aviation in the summer of 1916. Some barnstormers staged an exhibition near the family's Bristow, IA, farm and they all went out to see the show. Nineteen-year-old Clayton caught the flying bug and was soon reading everything a farm boy could find on the subject. He eventually discovered the Heath Aeroplane Supply Company during a trip to Chicago and was spurred to build his own airplane.

Clayton built three airplanes between the winters of 1918 – 19 and 1922 – 23. The first two, powered respectively with a 7-hp Indian motorcycle V-twin and a 13-hp Spacke V-twin cyclecar motor salvaged from a boat, didn't fly. The third, powered by an uncooled Model T Ford engine, was capable of brief hops. In sub-zero weather, the plane could fly for a minute or so before the engine overheated.

Folkerts' fourth design was an attractive shoulder-wing monoplane employing the then little-known geodetic method of construction. Folkerts fashioned a light and extremely strong fuselage of thin plywood strips woven together like a basket. He installed a two-cylinder, 28-hp Lawrance Penguin engine purchased from war surplus. The sturdy little plane resisted the Lawrance engine's serious vibrations and performed surprisingly well.

Wishing to develop a two-place version for production, Clayton Folkerts flew it to Dubuque during the summer of 1926, where he hoped to find financial backing. Here he met a Jenny pilot, Milt Miller of the Miller-Palmer novelty company, who was engaged in promoting a municipal airport. Miller was impressed with Folkerts' midget airplane and arranged for some publicity in the local paper.

That fall Milt Miller learned of Don Luscombe's project and of Lus-

Self-taught airplane designer Clayton Folkerts at Dubuque, IA, ca. 1926, with his fourth design. His next effort was to design an enclosed two-place for Don Luscombe's company, Central States Aero.

combe's pressing need for a competent designer and builder. Miller arranged for Luscombe and Folkerts to meet. As a consequence, Folkerts was hired by CSA for $35 a week. His one-year contract, effective November 1, 1926, was to "design, manufacture, study and experiment with aeroplanes" in accordance with the plans of the Central States Aero Company.

The Monocoupe takes shape

All Folkerts had to go on were Luscombe's cabin mockup, his enthusiastic word pictures, and an artist's rendering of the airplane. Don insisted on a steel tube fuselage. Accordingly, Folkerts borrowed an acetylene torch and taught himself to weld. The wing and its airfoil would be very important to the success of the design. Thus, they carefully studied a stack of NACA wing curve analyses and finally selected the popular Clark Y airfoil for the wing.

Another major challenge was to find a suitable engine for their design. War surplus OX-5 engines had dominated the market for years. Good engines at the lower end of the OX-5 replacement range were few. At first it appeared that the only practical production engine was the expensive French Anzani. But in 1927 two American engines were introduced that seemed promising. One was the 75-hp Kinner K-5. In the other instance, "Eddie" Rickenbacker and former Wright Field Chief Engineer Glenn D. Angle teamed up to make the five-cylinder 60-hp Detroit Air Cat. Luscombe bought an experimental Air Cat for $650 and ordered a propellor from Hartzell.

As the CSA project progressed at Wallace Field, Luscombe, ever the merchandiser, began to look for a catchy name. Milt Miller (Miller-Palmer Co.) was then manufacturing a toy glider called the "Mono-Kite" and the CSA airplane was being referred to frequently as a "flying coupe." Luscombe played with the words and came up with *Monocoupe*. It was perfect. The name was unanimously adopted as the official company trademark.

Folkerts completed the airplane late in March 1927 and Luscombe invited E.K. (Rusty) Campbell, operator of the Moline airport, to make the first test flight. Campbell took to the air for the apple-green prototype's milestone first flight on April 1. His laconic test report was prophetic: "Great future."

The facilities at Wallace Field were inadequate to manufacture airplanes. But the evangelist Billy Sunday had erected a capacious clapboard "tabernacle" on a corner lot in Bettendorf before moving on to greener pastures. Luscombe rented the building for $12 a week and hired a dozen shop hands. In May, work began on an initial batch of 10 airplanes.

CSA's Monocoupe was powered by a 55-hp Detroit Air Cat engine. A trio of "greats"—Eddie Rickenbacker, Glenn D. Angle, and Ivan Driggs—are shown here during development of the engine. Driggs built the Driggs Coupe "demonstrator" for Rickenbacker to showcase the Air Cat engine designed by former McCook Field chief engine designer, Angle.

The prototype Monocoupe at Wallace Field, April 1927. Folkerts built the plane single-handedly in 4½ months without blueprints or formal engineering. The all-moving rudder was superseded in production by conventional fin and rudder.

First production Monocoupes

The first production Monocoupe rolled out of the tabernacle in the summer of 1927. The Air Cat-powered Monocoupe weighed 749 pounds empty and carried a useful load of 475 pounds for a gross weight of 1224 pounds. Two 10-gallon fuel tanks were installed in the wings; wingspan was 30 feet. Folkerts had built the prototype with an all-moving tail, but this was superseded in production with a conventional fin and rudder. The plane's landing gear was of the axle-and-spreader-bar type with rubber shock cord to absorb the loads.

The single cabin entry door was located on the right side, but could be installed on either side on special order. Some liked to fly the throttle with the right hand, so they preferred the door on the left. This feature divided the airplanes into "left-hand" and "right-hand" Monocoupes!

The Monocoupe's two seats were slightly staggered to offer more shoulder room in the narrow cabin, and its occupants viewed the landscape below through large windows of pyralin. A "Berryloid" finish of various colors was optional to the customer. The first production Monocoupe sported a dazzling Berryloid finish of maroon with gold trim, doped and painted personally by Tom Colby, manager of the Aviation Division of Berry Brothers Paints.

The Monocoupe landed at 38 mph and cruised at a very decent 80 mph; at reduced power, its range could be stretched to 400 miles as advertised. Its price at the factory was originally $2275.

George A. Wies, the Stinson and Stearman distributor for the East Coast, obtained the first Monocoupe franchise. Wies took delivery of the first production Monocoupe at Wallace Field late in July and flew it back to his base at Curtiss (Roosevelt) Field, Long Island. Wies quickly spread the word about Monocoupes. For a while he displayed the first production aircraft at the Abercrombie and Fitch department store.

Dale Folkerts

Lineup of the first three Monocoupes at Wallace Field.

Col. Charles Lindbergh made a test hop in Wies' Monocoupe, then ordered one for himself. Lindbergh specified that the airplane be equipped with brakes (the Monocoupe had none), and Folkerts eventually found a type of motorcycle brake that was adaptable to Monocoupe wheels.

Another of CSA's early customers was a young North Dakota barnstormer, Vernon L. Roberts. Roberts, sponsored by the Fargo Aeronautic Club, entered his Monocoupe, *Miss Fargo*, in the 1927 New York-Spokane Derby. Unfortunately, his prop flew off halfway to his goal, ending his flight. (In subsequent years he would make far better showings.) Shortly thereafter, Luscombe hired Roberts as a test pilot.

Certification

As a result of the 1926 Air Commerce Act, all commercial aircraft produced after 1927 were required to be approved by the newly created Aeronautics Bureau of the Department of Commerce. Clayton Folkerts—Luscombe referred to him as "the farmer"—did not have the formal training to meet the government requirements for technical documentation.

Luscombe flew to Chicago and found a young consulting engineer named J. F. "Jerry" Lederer. Lederer was well qualified for the job of certification. An NYU graduate, he had been an assistant to Professor Alexander Klemin for a year, erecting and calibrating the university's new wind tunnel. Before

Jerome Lederer, ca. 1927. Don Luscombe hired Lederer, an experienced engineer, to provide the Department of Commerce with the technical data required to certify the Monocoupe.

becoming a consultant he had gained practical experience with the U.S. Air Mail Service in the repair and maintenance depot at Checkerboard Field near Chicago. Lederer hired two other graduate aero engineers, Fred Knack (also an NYU grad) and Bud Whelan. Lederer did most of the stress analysis, Whelan did the drafting and weight-control work, and Knack assisted with stress analysis and paperwork.

At the conclusion of the task, Jerry Lederer submitted the certification papers personally in Washington, DC, and stayed to answer questions. ATC #22 was issued to CSA in January 1928. The Monocoupe became the first light cabin monoplane to be certified for manufacture. Lederer then left CSA; Knack and Whelan stayed on.

Air Cat delivery problems

The production of Monocoupes proceeded briskly. But Rickenbacker's financially shaky enterprise, the Detroit Aircraft Engine Corporation, could not supply engines fast enough. CSA was building and selling Monocoupes faster than Air Cat engines could be produced. As a stopgap measure, Luscombe bought five 70-hp Siemens-Halske engines (a German radial) from their U.S. distributor, T. Claude Ryan. Some customers provided their own engines (60-hp Anzanis, for example).

Then Detroit Engine's fortunes went from bad to worse. When they hit rock bottom, CSA received a call from Detroit: "We've got one of your motors on the test stand. Better pick it up quick before the sheriff gets it. The plant's shutting down for good tomorrow afternoon!" Luscombe drove all night and grabbed his last Air Cat engine the next morning.

Velie Motors

CSA's pressing need for a steady supply of engines and for more working capital prompted Luscombe to approach a local automaker, Willard L. Velie, Sr., in January 1928. General Motors had made deep inroads into Velie Motors' share of the auto market and much of the Velie factory was idle. Luscombe persuaded Velie to undertake production of a reliable engine for the Monocoupe and to bankroll Luscombe's struggling enterprise. The Velies, father and son, visited the Bettendorf Tabernacle and inspected the Monocoupe assembly line there. The Velies were "sold" and within the week Central States Aero became Mono Aircraft, Inc., a property of the Velie Motors Corporation. Don Luscombe became vice president and sales manager of Mono Aircraft. Soon afterward the operation moved to a more satisfactory location at Moline's Tri-Cities airport.

Producing the Velie engine

Mr. Velie immediately requested one of the Rickenbacker motors. However, the last Air Cat Monocoupe had been sold to John Livingston of Monmouth, IL. Livingston, in turn, was about to deliver it to Fred Foote of *Life* magazine. Luscombe, accompanied by Frank Wallace (and six bottles of Wallace's best scotch), raced the 50 miles to Monmouth. Hours later they finally persuaded Livingston to return the Monocoupe. Livingston flew it back to Moline the next day, arriving at four in the afternoon. By 9 P.M. the Air Cat engine was being dissected by Velie's engineers.

The first Velie M-5 was running in less than 30 days. They copied the Air Cat's design so closely that Velie Motors eventually had to pay damages in a patent suit. Unfortunately, the Velie engine also duplicated many of the Air Cat's shortcomings.

Doug Harris flight-tested the engine in March. It ran hot and rattled constantly from detonation. The early Velies dropped so much cast iron on Moline's Tri-Cities Airport that Rusty Campbell, the manager, complained that it was ruining his mowers. Velie agreed with Luscombe that the engine needed aluminum heads. Velie solved the cooling problem by providing sodium-filled valves as well as the aluminum heads.

Model 70 Monocoupe salvaged in 1956 by John Underwood and rebuilt by retired Lockheed chief test pilot Tony LeVier. The Monocoupe 70 was produced in Moline, IL, by Mono Aircraft, Inc., a division of the Velie Motors Corporation. It was the best-selling lightplane in the U.S. during 1928.

Carburetion was another headache. The early Velies used Zenith carburetors with weak float arms. Bumpy landings played havoc with fuel metering on the next takeoff, resulting in one forced landing after another. Finally, Mr. Velie made a dramatic plea to the management of Stromberg Carburetors for a reliable carburetor design. Stromberg accepted the challenge and soon developed an excellent carburetor.

As soon as the Velie engine attained production status, the Velie-powered version of the Monocoupe was certificated in September 1928 (ATC #70). As in the original instance, the airplane was designated the Model 70 after its ATC number. The Velie Monocoupes subsequently had a very satisfactory production run. Altogether, 350 Velie Monocoupes were built, the last in 1931.

Monocoupe's reputation grows

Under Don Luscombe's guidance the Monocoupe soon became very well-known. It was promoted in national competitions, was heavily advertised, and it soon had an excellent distributor network.

In July two Model 70s participated in the grueling 6300-mile 32-city Ford Reliability Tour of 1928. Mrs. Phoebe Fairgrove Omlie (the first woman to hold a "Transport Pilot" license in the United States) finished in 24th place with her Monocoupe *Chiggers*. Jack H. Atkinson finished 19th. The instant popularity of the spunky little lightplane was clearly shown when Atkinson was awarded an additional $1200 for giving the greatest number of passenger hops flown at stops along the way. That fall Vern Roberts flew his Monocoupe, *Little Sweetheart*, one of two Monocoupes entered in the 1928 National Air Races (NAR) held at Los Angeles. The Velie-powered planes acquitted themselves well flying against competitors powered with engines of 90 hp and more.

In August, shortly before the Model 70 was certificated, Don Luscombe's fertile mind devised yet another effective promotional scheme. Luscombe had written a 54-page booklet, *Simplified Flying*, which he described as "a non-technical review of salient points in primary flying." Luscombe, the advertising pro, then prepared a colorful double-page spread with a clip-out coupon offering the booklet for 10 cents. The advertisement appeared in *Liberty*, a leading biweekly, and precipitated an avalanche of dimes—19,000 responses. The company had to hire extra help to handle the mail. After that, Monocoupe was practically a household word with thousands of air-minded Americans.

And the distributorships had expanded very nicely. By midyear, Mono Aircraft had established an excellent coast-to-coast network of distributors, extending from Geo Weis' in New York to John Hinchey's at Mines Field in Los Angeles. There were now 22 distributorships in the United States and two abroad.

Willard Velie, Sr., dies

During 1928 Mono Aircraft developed a four-place design to add to its stable. The airplane design was matched by a much more powerful Velie engine, designed by A. R. Weigel. The L-9 capitalized on the success of the M-5 engine, which had gained a good reputation and was beginning to be used on aircraft of other makes. The L-9 was a 180-hp, nine-cylinder radial intended to power the four-place. Only two years after the founding of CSA, Vern Roberts made the maiden flight on October 24. On the evening of the same day, Willard Velie, Sr., died at his home in Moline at the age of 62.

Despite the loss of the elder Velie, 1928 had been a year of substantial gain for Mono Aircraft. During the year the company had produced approximately 275 Monocoupes. By the end of that year the Bureau of Aeronautics had granted Type Certificates to 39 builders for nearly 100 aircraft types. Remarkably, at that time 10 percent of *all* licensed aircraft in the United States were Monocoupes!

Even more successes lay ahead.

The classic
Monocoupes

The year 1929 was a momentous one for Mono Aircraft Corporation. The company expanded its product line substantially, obtaining ATCs (Approved Type Certificates) on six new designs. And early in the year, the untimely death of Willard Velie, Jr., (less than half a year after his father's passing) caused a significant reorganization of the company.

The first of Mono's new models to be introduced in 1929 was the Model 113. The Model 113 (ATC #113) was basically an improved Model 70 and was powered by the same Velie M-5 engine. The significant improvements consisted of a new split-axle landing gear and longer wings. The split-axle landing gear was made up of two long oleo-spring legs that were connected to the upper fuselage. The legs, streamlined by long metal cuffs, were of fairly wide tread and long travel and made even a so-so landing feel like a good one. Wingspan was increased from 30 to 32 feet, which provided improved stability and somewhat better performance.

Death of Willard Velie, Jr.

The Monocoach (ATC #201), powered by the 220-hp Wright J-5, and the Monocoach 275 (ATC #275), powered by the 225-hp seven-cylinder Wright J-6-7, were Mono Aircraft's bids for the four-place market. The prototype Monocoach had first flown in the fall of 1928 with a 180-hp Velie L-9 engine. Development of the L-9 was abandoned and the Monocoach was certificated with the more satisfactory 220-hp Wright J-5. The improved Monocoach made its first flight on the 20th of March. By fateful coincidence, Willard Velie, Jr., suffered a heart attack the same day and expired within hours.

Introduced late in 1928, the Model 113 (ATC #113) Monocoupe offered split-axle landing gear, longer wing. Depression reduced price from $2,835 to $1,895.

The Velie business was folded into the John Deere tractor business, with which it had some connection. Velie's family sold the aircraft subsidiary to a hastily formed St. Louis holding company, Allied Aviation Industries. Don Luscombe became president and general manager of the reorganized Mono Aircraft Corporation. Concurrently, Velie Motors became the Lambert Aircraft Engine Corporation under Samuel B. Lambert, a partner in a St. Louis automobile agency who flew his own Monocoupe and liked to tinker with engines. Production of the Velie engine—now called a Lambert—continued

The Model 201 Monocoach was introduced in 1929. Mono Aircraft's entry into the four-place market was powered by the popular 220-hp Wright J5 engine.

under his direction. (As nobody but Mono Aircraft ever used the Lambert, when the Monocoupe finally became obsolete after 10 years of production, the Lambert died with it.)

Vern Roberts' 113 Special

Don Luscombe had hired Vernon L. Roberts in 1927 as his chief pilot in charge of test and development. Develop he did. In preparation for the 1929 racing season, Vern turned a stock Model 113 into a "Monocoupe 113 Special." He faired the airplane very carefully for more speed and nearly doubled the horsepower with the installation of a 110-hp Warner Scarab engine. He removed the standard Monocoupe wings and installed a set with elliptical tips and slightly reduced wing area (133.2 vs. 143 square feet).

Members of the 1929 Monocoupe racing team—Scotty Burmood, Florence Klingensmith, Phoebe Omlie, and R. C. "Stub" Quinby—did well with their new mounts. Phoebe Omlie, flying her new Monocoupe 113 Special *Miss Moline*, finished first in her class in the Santa Monica-Cleveland derby for women. She also won the featured women's closed-course race. Roberts and Quinby also acquitted themselves well in the 1929 NAR (National Air Races).

Jim Harvey

Phoebe Omlie, the first woman in the U.S. to hold a "Transport Pilot" license, was a marvelous "ambassadoress" for the Monocoupe. Omlie was a worthy member of the 1929 Monocoupe racing team. She raced her Warner-powered 113 Special, *Miss Moline*, to first place, flying from Santa Monica to Cleveland in the National Woman's Air Derby.

The Monosport I (110-hp Warner Scarab), developed from the 113 Special, doubled the horsepower of its predecessors and was soon seen on the racing circuit. This design introduced the elliptical wingtip that became the hallmark of all later Monocoupes.

New models

The Monosports, which were introduced that summer, were high-performance craft aimed at the sportsman pilot. Vern Roberts was largely instrumental in the developing of the Monosport series, a direct development from his 113 Special. The Monosport Model 1 (ATC #249) was powered by a 110-hp Warner engine. Its twin, the Model 2 (ATC #250), was powered by the popular five-cylinder Kinner K5 engine of 100 hp. These engine installations increased the power from 60 hp to a level that came to represent the definitive Monocoupe.

In mid-1929, Henry A. "Tony" Little bought one of the first Warner-powered Monosports for sport flying and air racing. In approximately three years time, Little and his Monosport competed in 87 closed-course races, finishing first in 51 events and second in 27 events. Tony Little was also a contender in seven cross-country derbies, taking first in three of them and second in two.

The Monoprep (ATC #218) was originally conceived during the 1928 NAR at Los Angeles, evolving out of discussions between Jack Frye and John Hinchey. Frye (later president of TWA) operated the Aero Corporation of California; Hinchey was Mono Aircraft's distributor for Southern California,

Jim Harvey

Success of Vern Roberts' Monosport, *Little Sweetheart*, on the racing circuit led to the development of the Model 90 (90-hp Lambert R-266), certificated April 1930. The design, fitted with a variety of engines, became the company's mainstay and endured until the demise of the Monocoupe Airplane and Engine Corporation in the late 1940s.

Arizona, and New Mexico. The result was an open-cockpit parasol-wing trainer version of the Monocoupe 113. The Type Certificate was granted on August 30, 1929.

Stock market plunges

The future looked bright for Don Luscombe's business. Sales were great. The company had built approximately 500 airplanes since the founding of CSA three years before. Monocoupes were winning cash prizes and trophies galore in all manner of competitions. Mono Aircraft had now developed a complete line of attractive products.

Then came the stock market crash of October 1929. On the 24th, over 12 million shares changed hands in a frenzy of selling; on the 29th came catastrophe. By the end of the month stockholders had suffered a paper loss of over 15 billion dollars. The outlook for Don's business changed dramatically.

Model 90

During that winter, Folkerts developed a new and vastly improved edition of the Monocoupe that reflected much of what had been learned from

Roberts' racing special and the Monosports. This was the Model 90, powered by the new 90-hp Lambert R-266. The prototype was rolled out of the experimental shop on January 13th, 1930, and made its formal debut at the International Aircraft Show at St. Louis on February 15th.

Compared to the previous Model 113 of 1929, this 1930 Monocoupe was a foot or so longer, at least 4 inches wider for more room in the cabin, and about 8 inches taller on its new-type landing gear. The wing spanned the same distance with new elliptical tips that cut down some on the area, and it weighed only some 10 pounds more when empty.

Mono Aircraft's classic Monocoupe had been born.

The Model 90 could be characterized as the quintessential Monocoupe. As such, it is appropriate to provide the little gem's vital statistics. Listed below are specification and performance data for the Monocoupe model 90 (1930-31) as powered with the 90-hp Lambert engine and incorporating a speed-ring cowling and engine starter:

Length overall 20 feet 10 inches; height overall 6 feet 11 inches; wingspan 32 feet 0 inches; wing chord 60 inches; total wing area 132 square feet; airfoil Clark Y.

Weight empty, 888 pounds; useful load, 631 pounds; payload with 30 gallons fuel, 266 pounds; gross weight, 1519 pounds; gas capacity, 30 gallons; oil capacity, 2.5 gallons.

Maximum speed 118 mph; cruising speed, 102 mph; landing speed, 40 mph; climb, 850 feet first minute from sea level; ceiling, 15,000 feet; cruising range at 5.5 gallons per hour, 500 miles.

Price at the factory was $3375, lowered to $2885 in 1933.

Setbacks

During this period of time Curtiss-Wright was conducting an aggressive expansion program that resulted in a severe marketing setback for Mono Aircraft. The Curtiss-Wright Flying Service—then the exclusive agency for Cessna, the deHavilland Moth, Curtiss-Robertson, Commandaire, Travel Air, and other C-W productions—bought out most of the best Monocoupe dealers. Luscombe had to go into the field and rebuild his sales and service network.

Other setbacks, more private and less disastrous, occurred. Sam Lambert was flying his Monocoupe to the All-American Aircraft Show in Detroit. Lambert carried with him the company's new little 35-hp "twin." It had just been successfully bench-tested and he intended to display it at the show. Near South Bend Airport, Sam made an exuberant power dive from 4,000 feet. Suddenly one of the metal propeller blades snapped at the hub; centrifugal force wrenched the motor from its mount, and the plane looped once and plunged nose-first into the ground. Sam was killed instantly.

Model 110

Back at Mono Aircraft, new developments went forward. The success of the racing specials prompted Mono to adapt the Model 90 to take the 110-hp Warner. Approval of the prototype Model 110 was obtained in June 1930. The plane was purchased by an Englishman, Lord Carberry, who flew the airplane the very next month in the grueling two-week Challenge de Tourisme International. He placed sixth in a field of 60 planes from eight nations. The Monocoupe would have won easily had it not been for the "roadability" test. Lord Carberry and his mechanic dismantled the airplane as required within the allotted time, but the wing proved too heavy to be fastened broadside on the fuselage for towing. All the winners had folding wings.

That same summer Vern Roberts and Johnnie Livingston each bought a 110. Between them they brought everlasting fame to the model with their 110 Specials. Their Monocoupe 110s were otherwise strictly stock machines, but they were powered by the improved Scarab series engine of 125 hp and

Jim Harvey

Johnny Livingston stole the show at the 1931 National Air Races with his modified Monocoupe 110 (125-hp Warner). Livingston's 149.46 mph bested the 142.2 mph of competitor Vern Roberts.

cowled with a narrow-chord Townend speed-ring. Their planes topped out at about 135 mph. At the 1930 NAR held at Chicago, Vern Roberts and his Monocoupe *Little Sweetheart* won many of the events and Livingston usually hung on for a close second.

The depression

Monocoupe racers such as Roberts' and Livingston's dominated the racing scene. Commentator Cy Caldwell quipped that the National Air Races ought to be called the National Monocoupe Races. Mono types placed first in 11 out of 15 events in which they were entered, second in 10 and third in nine. They also placed first in three cross-country derbies and claimed 63 percent of the total prize money posted for the events entered. Phoebe Omlie's winnings came to $3,250, Johnny Livingston pocketed $2,900 and Vern Roberts $2,850. The earnings of Bart Stevenson, J. Wesley Smith, Stub Quinby, Tony Little (Monosport), Marty Bowman, Gladys O'Donnell, and Scotty Burmood ranged from $425 to $1,300. At a time when the national hourly wage was about 50 cents, this was big money.

The racing scene gave a false picture of Mono Aircraft's fortunes. The depression had resulted in a precipitous drop in Mono's sales and earnings. As winter approached, Monocoupe production was sharply curtailed. Early in 1931, Mono Aircraft and Lambert Engines were placed in the hands of a receiver, Robert A. Cole, the result of friendly action initiated by creditors within the industry. The court directed Cole to continue operating the company as a going concern. Don Luscombe obtained backing in the amount of $50,000 and tried to recover control. The sale was denied, however, when the creditors insisted on payment of the full $78,000 purchase price.

Rescue

The company received a new lease on life when it became the property of Phil deCameron Ball of St. Louis. Ball had made a fortune by inventing the first practical ice maker and he had plants all over the East. He had been a silent partner of Lindbergh's in 1927 and owned, among other things, the St. Louis Browns and most of Ryan Aircraft. Mono Aircraft moved into the former Ryan plant at Lambert Field, near St. Louis, and commenced operations under its new name, The Monocoupe Corporation, on August 1st, 1931. Once again Don Luscombe was at the helm.

When the company moved to St. Louis, Folkerts left the firm and went on to fame as the designer of small high-performance racing planes. Frederick Knack replaced Clayton Folkerts as chief engineer. Manufacture of the Lambert engines continued at Moline.

1931 Nationals

Meanwhile, Johnny Livingston had decided to eat Vern Roberts' dust no more. He keenly wanted to be Number One. Thus motivated, he initiated a thorough aerodynamic cleanup of his aircraft. He installed a new faired landing gear, added streamlined cuffs at all strut junctions, enclosed the wheels in

Livingston's 110 Special as it appeared in Miami, January 1933. The Warner engine had been uprated to 145 hp, and the standard wheels (see above) had been replaced with 8-inch racing gear. NR 501W was then turning in racing speeds exceeding 170 mph.

Engineer Fred Knack with prototype 90A. This model introduced wing flaps and the Watters tunnel cowl in 1934.

wheel pants, redesigned the carburetor air scoop, and faired all protruding nuts, bolts, and fittings to cause the least disturbance to the airflow. He also tested and installed a special engine fairing. By the time of the 1931 NAR at Cleveland, Livingston's 110 Special was doing 186 mph!

Johnny Livingston stole the show at Cleveland with his racing Monocoupe. He won six speed events and placed second in two other races. He also won three deadstick landing contests and flew off with a grand total of $6,180 in prizes.

Howard DGA

Shortly after the 1931 races, Benny Howard hitched a ride to Chicago in Livingston's Monocoupe. Howard already had one successful racer to his credit and was building two more at Kansas City. The Monocoupe's speed astounded him.

"I don't know what makes this thing so fast," Howard told Livingston, "but someday I'm going to build one just like it with the biggest engine I can find!"

True to his word, Howard started detail design of the DGA-6 in September 1933; it was intended to be a racing machine as well as a commercially marketable aircraft. He built the plane in the American Eagle factory building across the street from Kansas City's Fairfax Airport (where Don Luscombe, "father" of the Monocoupe, and Ivan Driggs were designing and building the Luscombe Phantom). Howard installed a 500-hp Pratt & Whitney Wasp Senior engine. His DGA-6, christened *Mr. Mulligan*, was completed in June 1934. The following year, *Mr. Mulligan*, the oversized Monocoupe, won the 1935 Thompson Race (piloted by Harold Neumann). It also won the 1935 Bendix Race (flown by Howard himself)—the only aircraft ever to take *both* races!

1932 Nationals

Livingston continued to modify his airplane for more speed. He calculated the minimum wing size to attain the ideal wing area for racing, i.e., small enough to minimize form drag and large enough to minimize induced drag. He ordered the resulting 23-foot wing from the Mono factory along with a new tail group of reduced area and span and installed a 145-hp Warner engine. He used smaller wheels, made a major change in the windshield shape, and continued his experiments on engine cowling. Livingston streamlined everything and polished every surface. Finally, he employed a jet-type exhaust to obtain extra boost. As a result, his racer's top speed was increased to 220 mph.

Jack Wright's 110 Special

Early in 1933, John H. "Jack" Wright acquired Livingston's 110 Special. The airplane was sent back to the factory for further refinement and reappeared at the American Air Races in Chicago with an Approved Type Certificate (2-452) and the name *Baby Ruth*. Wright placed first in three ATC speed events, netting over $2,600 in cash awards. On July 5th, the final day of racing, *Baby Ruth* made an unofficial world's speed record of 180.47 mph for aircraft under 1,000 pounds. Six months later at Miami, Wright established an official world's speed record of 169.9 mph with a passenger. Late the following year, Wright and copilot John Polando flew the airplane in the sensational MacRobertson London-to-Melbourne race. In January 1935, Miss Helen MacCloskey of Pittsburgh averaged 166.67 mph over the 100-kilometer course at Miami to set a lightplane speed record for women in Wright's *Baby Ruth*.

Model D

Monocoupes were built for pilots of average size. It took a shoehorn for big pilots such as George Wies (6 feet 4 inches), a Monocoupe distributor, to get into one. The Model D was an attempt to address that problem.

Fred Knack designed the D-model in the winter of 1931 – 32. He designed it with a cockpit that was fully six inches wider than the Model 90/110. But apart from the wing, which was built in two panels to gain headroom, the airframe was essentially the same as the standard Model 110.

In December 1932, Don Luscombe hired noted designer Ivan Driggs as his chief engineer. Driggs was particularly known in the field for two of his lightplane designs, the Driggs Dart and the Driggs Skylark. A few months later, Ben Melcher was also hired by the firm. Melcher, along with Driggs, would figure in Don Luscombe's subsequent venture.

Development of the D-model continued in 1933 under Driggs' direction. A second prototype was built around the new 145-hp Warner Super Scarab. It was better streamlined and featured a number of refinements hitherto reserved for the racing specials. Luscombe demonstrated the D-145 in the East during the summer and booked several orders. But in the depths of the Depression, the prospects for future sales looked slim.

For some time Luscombe had been cogitating on the future of lightplane design. He had persuaded himself that this future lay with all-metal construction. Metal airplanes with fuselages of monocoque construction began showing up in the U.S. at the very beginning of the decade. John K. "Jack" Northrop had designed and built an all-metal passenger-carrying mailplane,

Monocoupe D-145 (145-hp Warner Super Scarab) was upsized by designer Fred Knack. The cockpit was 6 inches wider than Model 90/110; wing constructed in two panels. Ivan Driggs continued development after Fred Knack left the company. Driggs then resigned in October 1933 and went with Don Luscombe to Kansas City to design a lightplane of metal.

the Alpha. Boeing had built the all-metal Monomail and had followed it with the Boeing 247 10-passenger transport. Now, in mid-1933, this design was in service with United Air Lines. Douglas had designed a competing passenger transport, the DC-1, for Transcontinental & Western Air. To Luscombe's mind, metal construction for airplanes was the wave of the future.

Then the company's "angel," Phil Ball, died. That was a severe blow. With Ball gone, the company and its backers probably had neither the will nor the resources to undertake a difficult new development.

Don Luscombe felt that it was time to make his next move. He resigned later in October and headed west across Missouri to Kansas City with his chief engineer, Ivan Driggs, to build an all-metal lightplane.

3

The Phantom

America's first metal lightplane was born in Kansas City. Conceived by Don Luscombe and engineered by Ivan Driggs, it was a pace-setting addition to the American aviation scene. Don Luscombe linked his pioneering effort to build a metal lightplane with yet another idea. He intended to test his belief that airplanes could be built *without a factory*.

Luscombe set up shop at the Kansas City Municipal Airport in the Butler Aircraft building, where the Blackhawk biplane had been built. (The building is still standing and is used today by the Aero Mechanic's school.) Don used the same facilities and equipment that A. K. Longren had used to develop a metal monocoque fuselage. Longren had gone bankrupt, and Luscombe acquired Longren's hydraulic stretch press for virtually nothing.

Luscombe asserted that: ''Unfortunately the welded steel tube-fabric-ferring-sheet metal-wood combinations in aircraft have required large multi-department factories with a subsequently large manpower and costly administration. The better equipped the factory, the larger the burden.'' Don believed that the conventional method of aircraft construction was too costly. He decided to restrict his activity to the assembly of parts manufactured by firms that specialized in their manufacture. By adopting metal construction, Luscombe believed that it would only be necessary to manufacture his own dies, and then any stamping concern could stamp out the parts. The stampings would then be delivered to the factory to be heat-treated and fabricated. In this manner he believed that production costs could be reduced to a minimum.

Instrument panel on Doug Combs' flawlessly restored Phantom, 272Y.

Don Luscombe moved from Kansas City to West Trenton, NJ, in early 1935 and began building Phantoms on the floor of an 80 × 100-foot hangar. Ralph Coston, later foreman of the detail parts department, begins the construction process at a drill press.

Detail parts department (background) and welding department (foreground) were located at the back of the hangar.

Phantom design

Late in 1933, Luscombe and Driggs began to turn a dream into reality. Ivan Driggs designed the Luscombe Model 1 with a graceful metal fuselage incorporating compound curves. When the factory's sheet-metal workers had mastered the Longren hydraulic stretch-press, Luscombe and Driggs assumed that fabricating the fuselage parts would be quick and inexpensive.

Driggs, ably assisted by Lyle Farver and Ben Melcher, proceeded steadily with the design. But Don's bold idea of machine-built airplanes was shredded before his very eyes. Longren's stretch-press was better at tearing up sheet metal than it was at sculpting the graceful compound curves built into the dies. It destroyed about nine out of every ten fuselage skins.

Don finally admitted defeat and went out to hire the best sheet-metal man he could find. He hired Nick Nordyke, an unemployed sheet-metal worker. Nick was born in Holland into a family of sheet-metal workers. He was about six years old when he formed his first sheet of copper. Don's choice was unexcelled. "You could give Nick a penny and he could make it into anything you asked him," a coworker later related.

Forming the fuselage skins laboriously by hand escalated the cost. And—unfortunately—no one else could duplicate Nick's craftsmanship. But Nick Nordyke saved the program.

Fuselage assembly began in metal jig along one side of the hangar.

Loren Bump

The Luscombe Phantom

Late in the spring of 1934 the airplane was completed. The finished airplane that rolled out of the hangar was a thing of beauty. The Model 1 was resplendent in a shiny coat of cream-colored paint enhanced by a brilliant stripe of red trim along its fuselage. Understandably, it bore a strong family resemblance to Mono Aircraft's Model D-145.

The all-metal fuselage framework was a stressed-skin monocoque structure of 17ST dural bulkheads covered in .065-inch Alclad metal sheet. (By comparison, the skins of the Cessna 172 fuselage are only .025 inch thick). The thick skins resulted in an exceptionally strong fuselage.

"To make sure of our figures for strength on this type of structure," wrote Luscombe, "we piled 18,000 pounds of sand on the fuselage without a wrinkle."

The all-metal wing structure was built up of extruded dural I-section spar beams with stamped-out dural wing ribs. The leading edge was covered with dural metal sheet and the completed framework was covered in fabric. A 16½-gallon welded aluminum fuel tank was installed in the root end of each wing half. An elaborate fairing joined the wing to the fuselage.

Completed right-hand wing of Phantom ready for covering.

Stainless-steel split flaps were installed under the wing ahead of the aileron hinge line; their operation was electrical or manual. The flaps stretched across the greater portion of the wingspan, overlapping the high-aspect ailerons. Luscombe asserted that they had little or no detrimental effect on the lateral control, the spillover leaving the aileron pressure effective at the slowest speeds. The flaps required no further attention after switching on their small electric motor, which stopped automatically when the flaps had moved sufficiently. The flaps reduced the landing speed below 45 miles per hour and could be engaged when the machine was in a terminal velocity power dive.

The tail group was a composite structure; fixed surfaces were a riveted dural structure covered in Alclad sheet, and movable surfaces comprised a welded steel framework covered in fabric. Movable surfaces were aerodynamically balanced and the horizontal stabilizer was adjustable in flight (the trim crank moved the whole tailplane).

In addition to the flap motor and the landing lights mounted in the wings, a broadcast band radio set, electric starter, navigation lights, and an engine-driven generator were fitted as standard equipment.

The cleanly designed semi-cantilever landing gear of rather narrow tread consisted of two oleo legs braced with streamlined steel wire and mounted 6.50×10 low-pressure wheels and tires. The landing gear was completely faired with metal cuffs and fillets. Landing loads were absorbed by oildraulic (without shock cords) struts with a $5\frac{1}{2}$-inch deflection.

Structural integrity of the stabilizer was checked by loading it with sandbags.

The tailwheel assembly combined lightness with simplicity. The combination of a leaf spring supported by a vertical member with rubber discs carried in the fuselage allowed the use of a small, low-drag, rubber swivel wheel that would neither shimmy nor puncture.

Entrance to the roomy cabin was provided through two large unobstructed doors. The 42-inch-wide cabin seated two side-by-side on thick, spring-filled cushions covered in leather. An 8-cubic foot baggage compartment behind the seat back had allowance for 66 pounds. A large curved windshield and Pyralin side windows, plus rear quarter windows and a skylight, offered good visibility in all directions. The ventilating system had been designed to make possible careful regulation of cabin temperature while keeping it safe from engine fumes.

The Phantom was offered with a Warner engine of either 125 or 145 hp (at 2050 rpm) enclosed in a Watters tunnel cowl. This cowl also offered the added feature of accessibility to valve adjustment and engine accessories. With the 145-hp Super Scarab engine, the Luscombe Phantom was to be sold for approximately $6000.

Phantom specifications

Listed below are the advertised specification and performance data for the Phantom I as powered with the 145-hp Warner Super Scarab engine:

Length, 21 feet 6 inches; height, 6 feet 9 inches, wingspan, 31 feet; wing chord, 62 inches; total wing area, 132.5 square feet; airfoil, NACA 2412.

Weight empty, 1320 pounds; useful load, 630 pounds; payload, 236 pounds (one passenger and 66 pounds baggage); baggage, 66 pounds; gross weight, 1950 pounds.

Maximum speed, 168 mph; cruising speed, 142 mph; landing speed (with flaps), 45 mph; climb, 1400 feet first minute from sea level; service ceiling, 19,000 feet; cruising range, 560 miles.

Gas capacity, 33 gallons; oil capacity, 3.5 gallons.

Price at the factory, $5995.

The prototype Phantom first took to the air on May 1, 1934, with Don Joseph at the controls. Don Luscombe knew and trusted Joseph and had invited him to come over from St. Louis to conduct the all-important first flights. Following those initial flights, Don Joseph returned to St. Louis and the flight test chores were then undertaken by Bart Stevenson, who operated a flying service in Kansas City. Ben Melcher also assisted in the flight test program during the development of a satisfactory engine cooling system. Bureau of Air Commerce identification number 272Y was assigned to the prototype and the Phantom 1 was granted an Approved Type Certificate (#552) on August 18. The Phantom made its public debut that fall at the National Air Races at Cleveland.

Work was begun on three more airframes, one of which was completed in December. NC275Y (serial number 101) was purchased by one of Luscombe's investors, the renowned Monocoupe pilot, R. L. "Pete" Brooks.

There was a serious problem with Luscombe's Kansas City location. This was epitomized by the fact that Pete Brooks hung his hat at the prestigious Aviation Country Club, Hicksville, Long Island. Don's midwestern location placed him far from the east coast, where both his investors and his principal market resided.

Pete was quite influential among Luscombe's investors—both current and potential—and he persuaded Don Luscombe to move East. Don agreed. In the fall of 1934 an abandoned county airport was located at West Trenton. Don's old friend Jerome Lederer checked out the field, its facilities, and the terms, and gave the deal his "thumbs-up."

About 12 employees—nearly the entire work force—elected to make the historic move to West Trenton, NJ, with Don Luscombe. Several of them were to make enduring contributions to the Luscombe story at West Trenton: Chuck Burgess, Lyle Farver, Keith Funk, Ross Funk, Alfred "Fritz" King, Ben Melcher, and Nick Nordyke.

Luscombe employees and students assemble for group photo, summer 1936, in front of Ig Sargent's new Phantom.

Fritz King made the move driving Ivan Driggs' Model A Ford. He pulled a trailer that was loaded with Chuck Burgess' boat and the pieces of a Fleet biplane that Fritz was rebuilding.

Mercer County airport in West Trenton, NJ, had been idled by the Depression. Only a weatherman occupied the facility. The county officials were eager to have the airport occupied and productive again. The administrators made an attractive deal and Don happily accepted the offer. The facilities consisted of a 240-acre lighted airfield with a brick and steel hangar containing 8,000 square feet of floor space. A 24-hour weather bureau with Department of Commerce teletype service was located on the field. The landscaped property included an eight-room clubhouse with four-car garage on the airport, a tennis court, a skeet field, and conveniently located stables.

Luscombe signed a three-year lease for $500 per year. The property was tax-exempt and came with insurance paid. The Department of Commerce assumed the duty of patrolling the property, which precluded the need for Luscombe to include watchmen on his payroll.

Luscombe shut down the Kansas City operation in December and the exodus began. The prototype Phantom was ferried to New Jersey. The office, the small inventory of tools, dies, and heat treating apparatus, and the unassembled parts of two Phantoms were loaded onto one truck-trailer, which departed for the east coast. Through the winter of 1934–35 the dozen employees, some married and some single, dribbled into West Trenton over a period of several weeks.

Once settled in West Trenton, Ben Melcher took charge of construction of the permanent steel jigs and fixtures to replace the wooden ones abandoned in Kansas City. Soon the assembly of the Phantom parts from Kansas City began and by March, serial number 102 was complete. In April, number 103 was also completed.

That same month, the Luscombe Airplane Development Corporation (LADC) was incorporated with Ivan H. Driggs, Lyle L. Farver, Ben B. Melcher, and Ora May Luscombe as principals. Driggs, Farver, and Melcher held 100 shares each. Don's wife, "Brownee," held 1700 shares.

In a letter to potential investors, written shortly before the move to West Trenton, Don had stated: "We are assured and confident of selling at least fifty units of the $6000 model. . . ." The letter was wildly optimistic; Phantom sales were few and far between. Times were tough at LADC in the beginning, both for Luscombe and for the employees. Don paid the rent for the houses and apartments of some of the employees. The treasurer doled out money for groceries and other bare necessities. The rest of the wages and salaries consisted of IOUs from Luscombe. To Don, who carried the businessman's burden of meeting a payroll, the families of the married men were like "a bunch of hungry stomachs hung around my neck."

Most of those who made the trek from Kansas City hung on. Ivan Driggs, the chief engineer, didn't feel he could. LADC's prospects looked dim to him. Ivan despaired of ever receiving all of his back pay. In May, Driggs, the Phantom's designer, quit LADC.

Lyle Farver succeeded Ivan Driggs as chief engineer. But before Driggs left, he engineered a change to the landing gear in an attempt to improve the Phantom's tricky ground handling characteristics.

The Phantom's particular landing gear design made the airplane into a ground-loop just looking for a place to happen. The narrow tread was only part of the problem. More importantly, the oleo struts operated independently and behaved that way. One did not compensate for the other. Furthermore, wheel alignment was (supposedly) maintained by a sliding parallel rod mounted ahead of the main strut. This mechanism was only partially effective in preventing twisting of the landing gear under the loads from a wing-low landing. In an oft-quoted statement, Don Luscombe once said: "You could master the violin easier than the fancy footwork needed for avoiding ground-looping."

Ivan Driggs' attempt to stabilize the landing gear consisted of adding braces. A highly preloaded strut on each side stretched from a point high on the fuselage to the landing gear. The result was a barely perceptible improvement in handling.

Novices learn to build airplanes

During the summer of 1935, a young college student, Ignatius Sargent, wrote to Don Luscombe. Ig, a licensed pilot, had seen one of Don's picture postcards advertising the Phantom, and had become quite interested in the airplane. Eventually he visited the company at West Trenton and placed a $1000 down payment on a Phantom. Don couldn't demonstrate the plane to Ig. Not long before, Don had flipped the prototype onto its back while demonstrating it to the wife of Dr. K. Tschudi. NC 272Y was parked in the back of the hangar undergoing repair.

Ig Sargent, newly married, was planning on enrolling that fall in the Casey Jones School of Aeronautics. Don talked Ig out of that. "You'll learn an awful lot if you come down to Trenton and build your own airplane," Don asserted. And that's exactly what Ig Sargent did.

Ig Sargent, who helped build his own airplane, stands beside his pride and joy, NC 1286.

NC 1286 takes off from Mercer Field.

Ig started to work at Luscombe the first of September and was apprenticed to Fritz King. He commuted daily (weather permitting) from New York's North Beach airport (now the site of LaGuardia). Ig flew in his Monocoupe accompanied by his close friend, Eddie Davis, who had been offered an identical arrangement by Luscombe.

Throughout this period, LADC maintained a perilous financial existence. Ig, Eddie, and most of the other employees were living on Don Luscombe's IOUs. That fall it suddenly occurred to Luscombe that he could start a school. By formalizing the arrangement that he had with Sargent and Davis, Luscombe would be able to generate income for the company and to obtain a source of cheap labor for the factory.

Luscombe School of Aeronautics

The first small class was opened in January 1936. Bill Shepard, a Cornell graduate, was one of those enrolled.

Classroom space was initially provided by constructing quarters above the stockroom in the hangar. Don's supervisory personnel provided the classroom instruction and supervised the practical work being done on the factory floor.

Ig Sargent exuberantly buzzes the ramp in NC1286.

The idea worked very well and Don then received an okay from the Board of Directors to establish a formal school.

Students paid a tuition of $600.00 for six months of tutoring. Luscombe then paid the students cash salaries of $15.00 per week for six months in the shop and engineering departments. Luscombe calculated that 100 students would bring in $60,000 in tuition and would cost $39,000 in salaries, leaving a surplus of $21,000. Don wrote to his board of directors that "This means that since we have $2751.45 in our bill of materials we could stay in business without loss if we were to sell [Phantoms] at $2,751.45 rather than at our present price of $6,000.00—for all direct, indirect labor and general expense is carried by the school enterprise."

The second class, which began in early May, was better organized and had a larger enrollment. Approximately 50 men were enrolled, including graduates of Massachusetts Institute of Technology, New York University, Cornell and Michigan Universities. Eighteen held pilot's licenses.

The course of study for the school was devised by Prof. K.D. Wood, head of the engineering department at Cornell University. Operation of the school was conducted by C. W. "Cy" Terry, an engineering instructor in machine design on leave from Cornell, and P. E. "Penn" Muhlowney from North Carolina State. Terry also had pilot's and aircraft mechanic's licenses.

Lecture periods were conducted twice a day, with practical instruction continued on the shop floor where students participated in all types of work. Studies were included in design, stress analysis, production planning, stock control, cost accounting, and sales.

A housing problem soon developed in the vicinity of the airport due to the number of men enrolled. Many of the students stayed at a large old house nearby that had served as an inn. Its small rooms could accommodate some 30 students. Roger Johnson, the company treasurer, had obtained this accommodation; accordingly, it came to be known as "The Jolly Roger."

The Luscombe 90

Production of Phantoms proceeded at a very rapid pace in the last half of 1936. Luscombe's idea of a work-study program was working like a charm. Several dozen or more eager young students provided the shop with an increasingly skilled work force that boosted Phantom production tremendously. Eight Phantoms were built in the last half of 1936. Three of these were assembled in a single month, October, at the same time as the prototype of a cheaper version. From a production standpoint, at least, this period was the Phantom's finest hour.

But the Phantom was not an *affordable* airplane. Don badly needed an affordable design if LADC was to remain in business. So engineering went to work on one.

While the company was still in Kansas City, planning for the move to West Trenton, Don's business plan called for marketing two designs. Both the two-place and the four-place designs were planned to use three different engines. The two-place would use engines of 90, 125, or 145 hp (just as the Monocoupe had done). The idea of a 90-hp Phantom, the Sprite, was thus resurrected and engineering completed the design of a prototype in the early fall of 1936. The result was a stripped-down Phantom powered by a 90-hp Warner Scarab Junior engine. It used reworked Phantom wings with the flaps eliminated.

Fabrication of the Phantom fuselage was difficult because of the compound curves, which had to be hammered out by hand and required an expert (Nick Nordyke) to do it. For the 90 design, Lyle Farver and Ed Tarencz devised an improved method of fuselage construction that would lend itself well to mass production. The new fuselage design eliminated compound curves. The design was implemented by straight sections running from the cabin aft to the tail cone that could be flat wrapped around the contours of the ship on both top and bottom. These pieces did not meet in the center on the side when riveted to the bulkheads, causing a gap approximately 7

Phantom fuselage production line, early 1937. The fuselage of production prototype Model 4 (serial number 400) can be seen in the background.

Luscombe Model 4 production prototype with reworked Phantom wings from NC 272Y. Note the narrow-chord, full-span ailerons. The wings were redesigned for production Model 4.

inches wide on either side. This space allowed the jigs to be removed from the outside, rather than requiring an employee to climb inside to remove them as had been the method in Phantom construction. The aperture was then closed by riveting an 8-inch strip of dural to both the top and bottom shells. The dural had enough flexibility that it could be flexed away from the fuselage along the unriveted edge, leaving room to reach inside from the outside to buck the rivets. This too eliminated the necessity of having a person inside the fuselage, and would speed production with its efficiency.

The outline of the tail was also revised to blend with the lines of the fuselage. The sweeping curves of the Phantom tail were replaced by an attractive combination of straight lines and simple curves.

Landing gear

The Phantom's troublesome landing gear killed many sales. Apparently, only the most adept pilots could fly the airplane indefinitely without incurring an expensive ground-loop. Lyle Farver's design team planned to eliminate the problem on the Model 4. The engineers designed a single oleo strut for the 90 landing gear. The engineers tied the gear together under the floorboards, then attached this strut to an oleo cylinder in the center of the fuselage. By tying the gear together to a single strut, when one wheel dropped into a depression or hit a bump, the other wheel would move laterally, keeping the aircraft level. The gear was designed with sufficient rigidity so that flexing—another problem with the Phantom landing gear—would be eliminated.

Wings

The wings used the same extruded I-beams and ribs found in current production of the Phantom. Trailing edge flaps were employed and the wingtips were reshaped into a simple bow. All control surfaces were covered with fabric, as the Phantom's had been.

Ig Sargent first flew the prototype Model 90 on November 3, 1936. To his logbook entry Ig added the statement: "Not so hot." Nevertheless, Lyle Farver and his crew continued their work on the production version. By late January, mockup development had been completed and construction of the production prototype Model 90 began during the first week of February.

Enlarging the facility

The factory hangar was bulging at the seams in the fall of 1936. Students were crammed into the balcony rooms. There was a dramatic increase of

Ben Melcher takes a plaster cast of the side skin of the Model 4 fuselage for use in making drop-hammer dies.

airplane construction on the hangar floor. Don relieved the pressure by erecting three buildings immediately behind the hangar. A single-story building housed the new paint shop. Beside it was a two-story building that housed the Engineering department on the second story with the Sheet Metal shop beneath it. The last building in the row was also a two-story building, which housed the Luscombe school on the second floor with the school shop on the first.

Fritz King's "FBO"

The person who had assembled NX1017 was—as usual—Fritz King. Nick Nordyke was arguably the best-known of Don Luscombe's employees. One could probably say that Fritz King was equally well-known. Fritz King didn't have just one specialty; he had several. And he didn't just put in a good day's work for Don Luscombe. After hours he energetically pursued his own enterprises. In his words: "We weren't getting paid too good, you know. So I was always picking up a little extra cash."

Fritz King runs up the 100-hp Kinner engine on his newly rebuilt Fleet (brought in pieces from Kansas City). Tom Foley brings parachute to Fritz for first flight, which is imminent.

At one time or another, Fritz was Luscombe's chief wing builder (and repairer of Phantom wingtips!), chief installer (of engines, controls, and instruments), and chief test pilot. For a while he was the only one in the factory who knew how to splice cables. He also had the factory concession for the vending machines—cigarettes, candy, and gum. He was most visible, however, in his role as an in-house FBO at a company that was extraordinarily air-minded.

Fritz completed the rebuild of the Kinner-powered Fleet that he had hauled in pieces from Kansas City. As soon as the Fleet became airborne in the fall of 1936, he started instructing in it and running charter trips. The young apprentices at the school provided him with a steady stream of flying students. When a flying club was formed and an Aeronca C-3 obtained, he became one of the club's instructors. Fritz taught Don's wife, Brownee, to fly ("One of the best students I ever had."). He taught Frances "Cessie" Sargent, wife of the company's test pilot, to fly. Howard Jong and Ralph Coston helped Fritz to rebuild his Fleet, and Fritz paid them with flying lessons.

After Mercer County built an additional hangar for Luscombe's use, Fritz rented it from Don and, in turn, rented space to other local aircraft owners.

He soon found that his flying business was too much to run out of his hip pocket, so he erected a small building behind Jeff's hamburger shack to house it.

Fritz King's after-hours flying activities were a real success. His success suggested that there was something special about the people who were attracted to Don Luscombe and his factory. For the most part, they were nuts about flying. But they were generally people of modest means and, unfortunately, Don Luscombe was not building their kind of airplane.

4

Finally, a $2000 airplane!

"Frank, when are you coming? We need you. /ss/ Don Luscombe." Little did Don Luscombe realize, when he dictated those words to Lucy Rago, that he had set in motion a train of events that would transform the Luscombe Airplane Development Company.

Francis "Frank" Johnson responded immediately. For three years he had led a survey team for the National Forest Service. He had worked in all kinds of weather. He had waded in ice water up to his hips. He had just about had enough. The young engineer, a graduate of the University of North Carolina, went to work for Luscombe in July 1936. He was assigned to the sheet-metal shop under the incomparable Nick Nordyke. He quickly became very adept at shaping aluminum sheet—although *welding* the stuff was his nemesis. Indeed, Frank became so capable that Luscombe put him in charge of the sheet-metal shop and granted Nordyke a long-promised vacation to visit his homeland, Holland.

Later that summer, a new student, Howard W. Jong, was assigned to assist Johnson. Jong, a graduate of the Curtiss-Wright school in Glendale, CA, took to welding the aluminum gas tanks like a duck to water. From then on, Frank stuck to bumping aluminum and never welded aluminum sheet again.

Upon Nordyke's return, Frank was reassigned to the engineering department to take advantage of his engineering training. He was later reassigned to the Luscombe School of Aeronautics to replace Mr. Levy, the school's shop instructor, who had left, and was placed in charge of the school

Nick Nordyke (l.), master of forming sheet metal, and coworker, Frank Johnson. Later, while heading up Luscombe School of Aeronautics, Frank did predesign of a small two-place airplane intended to be built as a school project.

Howard Jong

Jerry and Lucy Coigny

Aerial view of Luscombe Airplane Development Company, spring 1937. Factory demonstrator NC 1048 and Model 4 (by autos) can be seen on ramp, and Fritz King's Fleet is in the background by the hangar. New outbuildings behind the factory are (l. to r.): paint shop, engineering/sheet metal shop, and classrooms/school shop.

in December 1936 when P. E. "Penn" Muhlowney resigned to return to North Carolina State. While he ran the school, Johnson continued to teach the technical subject matter—the fundamentals of aerodynamics, structures and materials.

After hours, Frank Johnson pursued an assignment that he had been given by Don Luscombe.

Phantom NC1048

Shortly before the model 90 production mockup was completed, Phantom NC1048 (serial number 116) rolled off the assembly line in mid-January. The plane was destined for exhibition at the 1937 New York Airshow, to be held January 28 through February 6. Following its completion, the shiny black Phantom was disassembled and trucked to the show rather than risking a first flight. Another exhibit at this same show was the new Aeronca K, which was making its debut there. The two-place Aeronca K was a light, strut-braced, high-winged cabin monoplane with side-by-side seating. Its two-cylinder Aeronca E-113-CB engine developed 42 hp. The all-fabric-covered airplane was constructed of the usual welded steel tubing fuselage and wooden wings. This sporty little plane and its steady stream of onlookers must have given Don Luscombe pause.

Predesign of the Model 50

On April 12, 1937, the company changed its name to the Luscombe Airplane Corporation, organized as a New Jersey corporation. Don was prepared to go public with the stock.

Meanwhile, a new idea was taking shape.

Cy Terry, his task of organizing the school completed, had returned to Cornell for the 1936 fall term. Penn Muhlowney was then put in charge of the Luscombe School of Aeronautics. Penn had wanted to build a quarter-scale Phantom as a school project. Muhlowney had wanted to keep everything to scale and had obtained 1/16-inch rivets and some sheet metal that was too thin for Luscombe to use for anything else.

Luscombe thought that the proposed project was a waste of valuable labor. He spoke with Johnson, who was in charge of the school now that Muhlowney was gone, about his reaction to the Muhlowney project: "Frank, we have all this cheap labor. We need something we can build a lot of; something like an Aeronca C-3. But it's got to be a side-by-side and look like an airplane." (The welded steel tube construction, fabric-covered Aeronca K, ATCed in April 1937, exemplified Luscombe's idea.)

First Model 4 (Luscombe 90), NC 1253 (serial number 400), runs up on ramp in front of the factory, April 1937.

Don Luscombe loved airplanes. He loved to sell airplanes, and he wanted badly to build one with more appeal. At this point he might even have considered building with welded steel tube and fabric. Phantom sales were far below his original expectations. Construction of the Model 4 production prototype was well along and already it was clear that the 90 was not going to solve his problem. He shared his view with Frank: "This 90 is no good. It's too expensive to just fly around the field. And for the price, it's too slow for cross-country work." In other words, it would appeal neither to the instructor pilot nor to the sportsman pilot.

Three-view

After work, Frank got out his drawing board and started sketching. The wing of the Aeronca C-3 had a 50-inch chord. One percent of chord was a very convenient 1/2 inch on the designer's layout. And this is what Frank chose. Johnson made a quick and dirty three-view drawing of an airplane with a 35-foot span, 50-inch chord, and NACA-4412 airfoil. He laid out the wing using the rear spar of the Phantom as the front spar of his 50-inch chord wing. For the rear spar he drew the rear spar of the Phantom with 3/4 inch cut out of

NC 1337 (serial number 403) as delivered to California-based Falcon Aircraft Corporation, August 1938. This aircraft, owned by Ron Price, Sonoma, CA, is the sole surviving example of its type. The plane is currently being restored.

the middle of the web and with the two halves spliced with two strips of .020 aluminum sheet riveted to the extruded web. He also drew a fuselage that was a squared oval in cross section.

Frank Johnson had been mulling over manufacturing ideas in his mind. He told Don his conclusion that the school-project airplane should be built of metal. Others could build "stick-and-rag" airplanes cheaper than Luscombe could. They couldn't build metal airplanes as cheap as Luscombe could. But Luscombe could build a metal airplane *as cheaply* as he could build a stick-and-rag airplane.

Don Luscombe concurred: "Okay, I'll give you an appropriation of $400. Get going."

Frank continued with the project. He laid out the cabin mockup, which extended from the firewall to about three feet aft of the seat. He laid out a 36-inch-wide seat with the cabin about 38 inches wide at the shoulders. An airfoil-shaped piece of wood, representing the wing root, was attached high up on the fuselage. When Frank's layout was complete he had the students build the mockup in the training shop using industrial plywood.

The narrow cockpit was unacceptable to Don Luscombe. "Frank, it doesn't matter whether you pay $6000 for the airplane, or $1600 for the airplane, your butt is just as wide." So Johnson changed the layouts and made the cockpit 40 inches wide.

NC 1344 at Aviation Country Club, Hicksville, L.I. Ig Sargent talks with Franklin T. Kurt (back to camera), who reported on the Luscombe 90 for the *Sportsman Pilot* (July 15, 1938).

The elliptical tips on the Phantom's wing were complicated to build—*too* complicated for a small, inexpensive airplane. So Frank drew a tapered leading edge at the outboard portion of the wing and a fairly straight tip between the spars. The ailerons, which were to be of metal, would be easy to make because the curved trailing edge would be simply "sewed up" with rivets.

Johnson then devised a simple way to build the ribs for a prototype. He made a Warren truss of 1/4-inch 4S aluminum tubing flattened on the inside of the bends (like lawn furniture). The students bent the tubing using a modified set of pliers that retained the round tube shape of the outer surface of the bend but collapsed the tube at the inner radius.

Johnson's job at the school kept him fully occupied there, so he did the engineering and the design layouts at night. At the time, he was living at the students' living quarters, the "Jolly Roger," as was Howard Jong. Jong visited Johnson's room often, observing the progress of the project with great interest. An apt and eager pupil, Howard soaked up the details and helped wherever he could.

Eventually the school project reached a point at which its promise was very evident to Luscombe. He instructed Johnson to turn the project over to Lyle Farver for further development by the engineering department.

Howard Jong had participated in Frank's school project from the beginning. Frank easily persuaded Don to transfer Howard into the engineering department. Farver decided to use Johnson's rib design concept to build the wing for the prototype of the "little" airplane. Naturally enough, Farver assigned Jong to the task of detail wing design.

The Continental A-50 engine

Frank Johnson had designed the school project airplane with a horizontally opposed ("flat") engine in mind. A new model of that type of engine now appeared. Early in 1937, Harold Morehouse, Continental's engineer in charge of small engine design, designed the A-50 engine. The A-40, which Continental then produced, was simple—probably the simplest four-stroke aviation engine ever built. It was a small (115 cubic inches) L-head motor with cast-iron cylinders, one-piece heads spanning two cylinders, single ignition, and only two main bearings.

By contrast, the A-50 at 171 cubic inches was larger than its competitors. It could deliver its 50 hp at only 1900 rpm. The A-50 was a real airplane engine throughout. Morehouse designed its cylinders like a radial's with steel forgings screwed into aluminum heads; the crankcase was a split aluminum casting. It featured a unique baglike steel oil sump suspended below the crankcase.

At that time it was common practice for engine manufacturers to promote an airplane design in order to showcase a new engine. Thus, early in July, a representative from Continental Aircraft Engine Company loaned a new A-50 dual ignition 50-hp engine to Luscombe to see if they would like to

(Left) Cabin mockup posed beside building housing Luscombe School of Aeronautics. (Right) School students constructed cabin mockup for Frank Johnson in school shop, using industrial plywood.

design an airplane around it. After some negotiation, Continental agreed to allow the company to use the engine free of charge until a type certificate could be obtained or for one year, whichever came first. Soon, therefore, the new design that was now emerging became known as the "50" to the Luscombe staff.

Mass resignation

Early in the summer, chief engineer Lyle Farver, Eddie Tarencz, and nearly all of the other engineers resigned. Sales of the Phantom, never high, were falling off. Sales prospects for the 90 looked dim. Employees were not receiving all of their wages and the several engineers left to seek greener pastures.

The company was dead without an engineering department. Don acted quickly. Fred Knack had first worked for Don when Knack helped Jerry Lederer obtain the ATC for the Model 22, the very first Monocoupe. Luscombe persuaded Knack to leave Douglas and return to Luscombe as chief engineer. He persuaded Jim Rising to leave Bellanca and become Don's chief designer. Knack quickly took control of the situation and the new design moved forward rapidly.

Design of prototype

Lyle Farver and Eddie Tarencz had concluded that few improvements could be made to the 90 fuselage. Consequently, except for shortening it by about six inches, they decided to use intact the tail cone and empennage of the 90 for the new design.

When Knack and Rising arrived, they affirmed Farver's design decisions on the aft fuselage and wing design. Their task was to design a complete new airframe from the tail cone forward. The main cabin was designed and its shape was faired into the shape of the tail cone. One result was a very awkward juncture between the trailing edge of the wing and the curve of the fuselage. Fixing the problem seemed to require an elaborate, expensive fairing such as had been used on the Phantom. Fred Knack decided to finesse the problem. He instructed Jong to design a simple notch into the trailing edge of the wing at the wing root. Flight tests would show whether the idea would work.

Large aircraft had been designed with control wheels in lieu of control sticks for many years. Now the latest Taylorcraft had come out with one, so the Luscombe engineers decided to build the 50 with a control wheel. The landing gear design on the Model 4 had been successful, so a very similar landing gear was incorporated into the 50.

Harold Neumann's 1941 bump-cowl Monocoupe 90A, "Little Mulligan," is painted to represent the Howard DGA "Mr. Mulligan." Neumann won the 1935 Thompson Trophy race with "Mr. Mulligan."

This attractive M36 Phantom, shown here in 1987 at Pioneer Airport, Oshkosh, Wisconsin, is on loan to the EAA Museum by the owner, George Ramin. The original owner of the NC 1025 was Luscombe investor Charles A. "Bunny" Hinsch.

Ron Price's Model 4 is the only surviving example of the type. This photograph (July, 1990) duplicates the view made at the time of the airplane's 1938 delivery.

This seldom-seen view of a float-equipped Luscombe was taken at Oshkosh, Wisconsin, during the annual EAA Convention in 1988. The 8F (converted from a 1946 8A) belongs to David W. Richardson and Kirt Elmschutz.

Ralph Boettner's 1948 8A in flight near its home base, Rockport, Missouri. This model incorporated all of the design improvements developed at Dallas; all-metal wing, simplified empennage construction, and Silflex landing gear.

The sharp, polished-metal 1948 8F shown here is owned by Eldon Iler. The photograph was taken in 1985 at the annual CLA fly-in at Columbia, California.

Bill Wright, San Diego, California, made a circuit in 1989 of the 48 contiguous states in his 1948 11A Sedan ("48 in a '48"). The plane is shown here in Arkansas during one of its stops.

This rare T-8F Army observation plane owned by Oakley Griffin appears in its Army uniform. The photograph was taken near Sonoma, California.

Howard Jong

The "Jolly Roger," a former inn near Mercer airfield, provided bed and board for many of Luscombe's students.

Howard Jong

Frank Johnson's room at the Jolly Roger. After hours, often accompanied by coworker Howard Jong, Frank made three-view drawings and calculated stress and performance for school project two-place plane.

Don was dubious about the Continental A-50 flat engine and insisted that the firewall be round to allow the use of an alternate radial engine should the A-50 prove undependable. Don also objected to the protruding engine cylinders of the partially cowled Continental A-40 engine used on the Taylor J-2 Cub and the Aeronca engine on the Aeronca K. He insisted that the engine on the 50 be fully cowled, as were the engines on the Phantom and the 90.

The nose cowl was the last section of the design to be worked out. Flat, horizontally opposed, air-cooled engines were relatively new. Pressure cooling of a fully enclosed flat engine had never been done before and the designers were unsure how to proceed. Nick Nordyke hammered out a trial configuration to give the team something to go on. He made a graceful faired cowl to cover the engine, with holes for the cylinders to protrude. Then he shaped separate air inlets, which attached to the cowl, to cover the cylinders. The four exhaust stubs protruded upward.

Pitcairn Autogiro contract

Engineering began another project in parallel with the design of the 50. Don Luscombe had brought in a much-needed outside contract during the summer. The Pitcairn-Larsen Autogiro Company of Willow Grove, PA, was starting to design the PA-36, an all-metal roadable autogiro. Luscombe obtained a contract to build the metal fuselage. Luscombe would also design all of the structure aft of the cabin. Bill Shepard had been working on wing design for the Model 4. When he had completed this task, Fred Knack assigned him to begin layout of the sheet-metal work on the Pitcairn autogiro.

Phantom production terminated

The introduction of the 50 project changed the direction of Don's future plans for the company. The engineers who had quit the company had envisioned a bleak future. But Don could see that a $2000 airplane held great promise. He proceeded confidently. On August 17, Luscombe signed a new 10-year lease for the factory site with the Mercer County Council. The area under lease was increased from 10 acres to 15.

About this same time a disappointed Frank Johnson left the Luscombe company. He had wanted to transfer to engineering when his airplane design project was turned over to Lyle Farver, but he was "stuck with the school." When the engineering department was rebuilt following the mass resignation of Farver and the other engineers, his situation remained unchanged. Then came an opportunity to design a low-wing metal airplane for a promoter. Frank took it.

Sheet-metal worker Howard W. Jong with NC 1253. Jong was soon transferred to engineering, where he did detail design of Model 8 wing.

Meanwhile, Don Luscombe made another milestone decision late that summer. He finally bit the bullet and decided to terminate production of the Phantom. When NC1265 (serial number 122) rolled off the assembly line in late September 1937, it became the last production Phantom. All subsequent Phantoms (there would only be three more) would be assembled from parts only after they had been purchased.

The company directors met on October 6, 1937, a few days after the rollout of the last production Phantom, and decided to increase capitol stock of the corporation, offering 145,000 shares for public sale at $2.50 per share. Don felt that the Luscombe Airplane Corporation had the potential of reaching volume production with the 90 and the new 50 if sufficient operating capital could be raised. The Board of Directors also voted to begin a dealership system after this date. Previously, all airplanes had been sold factory direct.

First flight

Ig Sargent first flew the prototype 50, NX1304, on December 21, 1938. The flight test program began in earnest after the beginning of the new year. These tests included an evaluation of the airflow past the notch in the wing

Chief designer Jim Rising teaches a class on technical subjects at Luscombe School of Aeronautics.

trailing edge. Carbon black in solution was applied to the leading edge of the wing at the wing root. During flight, the carbon black streamed aft and post-flight examination revealed that the smudges were smooth. No turbulence was evident; no fairing was necessary.

Cooling tests

As important as any of the flight tests were those conducted to develop satis-factory baffles for cooling the engine. The engineers thoroughly fitted the engine compartment with thermocouples. Fritz King flew the tests along with a passenger to record the temperature readings from the thermocou-ples. Time after time Fritz made full-power climbs at minimum speed. Fol-lowing each test the engineers would study the data, then rework the baffles to eliminate the hot spots. Continental's representatives watched the test results closely, and in the end everyone was very satisfied with the results.

Production prototype

The experience gained in building and flying the prototype suggested numer-ous worthwhile improvements to the design.

Johnson's school project design showed promise, was assigned to engineering, and the Luscombe 50 (50-hp Continental), NX 1304, resulted. The plane is shown here in the hangar shortly before rollout in December 1937.

NX1304's fuselage-mounted gas tank was mounted on the cabin side of the firewall. When the tank was full, the extra weight in the forward end of the plane had caused some center-of-gravity problems. Rising suggested placing the tank in the fuselage immediately behind bulkhead #3, suspending it from the upper fuselage with steel cables after the skin had been strengthened. Later service experience demonstrated conclusively that this mounting of the 14-gallon tank was secure and quite safe.

Luscombe 50 (Model 8) poses on ramp for publicity photo. Nick Nordyke crafted the cowl for the first example of a fully enclosed, flat horizontally-opposed engine.

The control wheel was replaced with a control stick. Ig Sargent and others who flew the plane didn't care for the wheel and much preferred a stick control. Don was very sensitive to customer reaction. He had visitors to the factory try out the wheel and they felt the same way. So the wheel control was abandoned.

The wing was redesigned for greater ease of construction. The engineers reverted to the tapered wing planform originally designed by Frank Johnson. New dies were prepared by the mill for the front and rear wing spars. The bent-tube rib construction, which had been a temporary expedient, was abandoned. In its place, a Vierindiehl truss construction was adopted. The main portion of the rib was built up of cap strips that were extruded dural T-sections bent to form the contour of the rib. Vertical truss members, made of 24 ST aluminum alloy sheet (cut to size and flanged), connected the upper and lower cap strips.

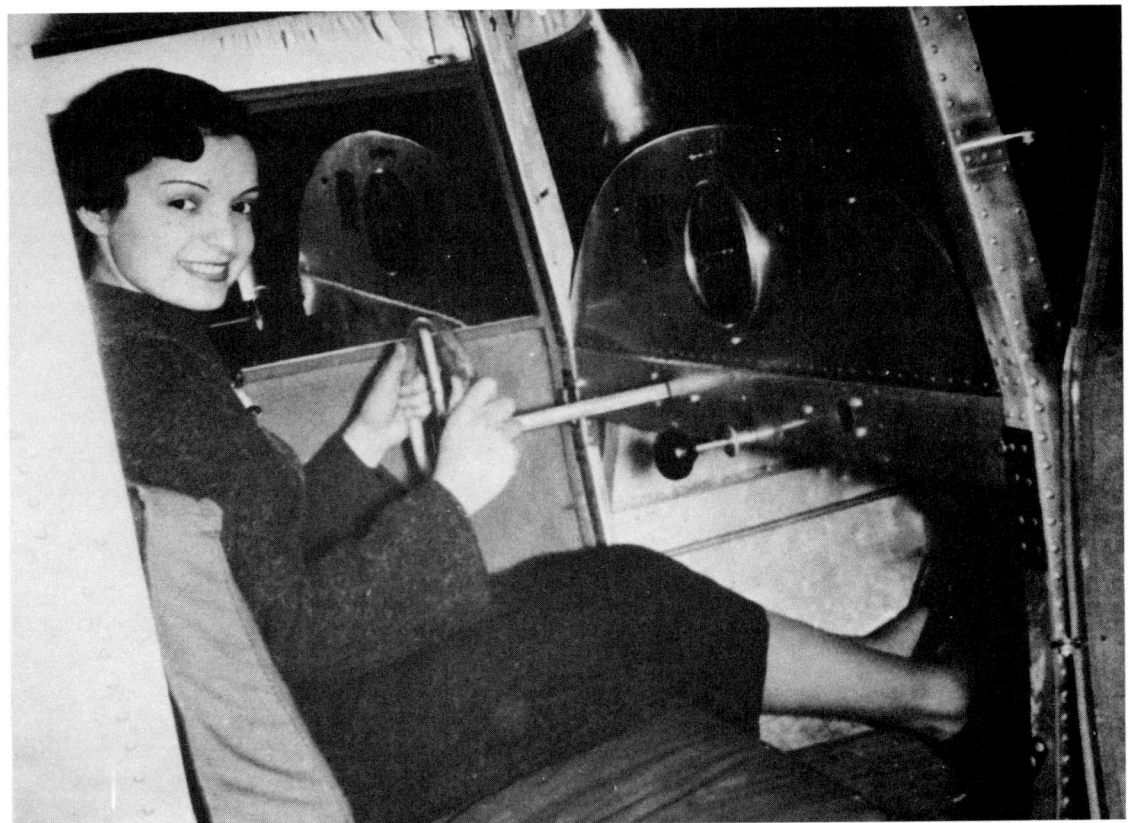

Loren Bump

Don Luscombe's attractive secretary, Lucy Rago, poses for another publicity shot. She demonstrates wheel control, which was originally provided on prototype 50.

The new wingtip was designed to fail without damaging the main spar, thus enabling an inexpensive repair to tips damaged in a ground-loop. The tip spars consisted of tapered 17ST Alclad channels, .065 in. thick. These were riveted to the extruded I-beam main spar and could be easily replaced.

The notch in the wing where the trailing edge met the fuselage remained. Ig Sargent's flight tests with carbon black had demonstrated that no aft fairing was required.

A distinctive new nose bowl and matching cowl replaced the original Nordyke version.

The fuselage tail cone of the prototype Model 8 was slightly shorter than that of the Model 4. Otherwise, it was a carbon copy. For the production Model 8, the engineers lightened and simplified the tail cone by deleting one bulkhead and relocating another to equalize the structure's load-carrying ability.

The fabric-covered control surfaces were replaced. Some students had visited the site of a wrecked Stearman-Hammond pusher, returning with an interesting artifact: a corrugated aluminum rudder. This idea for simpler, cheaper control surfaces was incorporated into the 50.

Model 4 production splurge

As the design on the Model 8 took shape, its promise became apparent. The Model 4 development was put on ice. By the spring of 1938 Don and the Board of Directors were looking ahead to production of the Model 8. They decided to make more room by cleaning house on the Model 4 and building three airplanes from the parts on hand. All three were completed in June and the ATC (#687) was granted on June 25, 1938, by George Gay of the Bureau of Air Commerce.

Model 4 specifications

Listed below are specifications and performance data for the fully equipped Luscombe Model 4 with the Warner Scarab Junior 90-hp engine turning a metal propeller:

Length, 20 feet 11 inches; height, 6 feet 6 inches; wingspan, 32 feet 1 inch; wing area, 140 square feet; airfoil, NACA 2412.

Weight empty, 1103 pounds; useful load, 622 pounds; payload, 258 pounds; gross weight, 1725 pounds; baggage, 60 pounds.

Maximum speed, 136 mph; cruising speed, 120 mph (at 85 percent power); landing speed (without flaps), 47 mph; landing speed (with flaps), 40 mph; rate of climb, 750 feet per minute.

Cruising range, 580 miles (at 85 percent power) with 30 gallons fuel.

Simple cockpit of Luscombe 90.

Model 8 production

First flight of the production prototype, NX1327, was conducted on June 6, 1938, by Ig Sargent. The tests went well and the CAA granted Approved Type Certificate #694 to the Luscombe Model 8 airplane on August 11.

While the flight tests proceeded overhead, production of the 50 proceeded briskly in the hangar below. Eager buyers were on hand before the first articles were ready to sell.

Falcon Aircraft of Los Angeles, a Luscombe distributorship owned by Carleton Darneal and Tom Warner, would take delivery of the second 50 that was available for domestic sale. The first production Model 8, serial number 802, had been shipped to France to be used as a demonstrator. Serial number 803 was spoken for by Jerry Coigny, a potential new west coast distributor who was associated with Falcon Aircraft. Carleton Darneal had flown four other pilots (including Coigny) across the continent in Falcon Aircraft's cabin Waco. They had flown to West Trenton to take delivery of four new Luscombes—a Phantom, a Model 4 (NC1337, serial number 403), and the two Model 8s.

Only one of the Model 8s was complete when the party arrived. This complicated matters since, except for Coigny, the pilots planned to fly as a group on the return trip. A couple of them were rather inexperienced and would be shepherded across the country. The situation was resolved amicably when Coigny relinquished serial number 803 and agreed to stay longer at West Trenton until serial number 804 was completed.

In-flight photo of first production Model 8, NC 1327 (serial number 801). Numerous changes were incorporated into the production version. Obvious external changes are redesigned tapered wings, redesigned engine cowl, and corrugated aluminum control surfaces.

Coigny, who had quit Douglas Aircraft only days before, was a skilled sheet-metal worker. He was also short of cash, so Luscombe readily agreed to hire him to help complete the construction of his own airplane!

Jerry Coigny soon noticed a photo on the bulletin board in the hangar. It was of a very attractive young woman seated in the prototype with her hands on the experimental control wheel. He learned that the young woman was Don's secretary, Lucy Rago. As soon as he was able, Jerry contrived to meet Lucy. His opening ploy was an offer for Lucy to be the first passenger in his new 50! They were soon dating.

Jerry Coigny accepted delivery of NC2591 (serial number 804) on August 17. The very next day he showed West Trenton to Lucy from the air.

Jerry immediately resurrected a defunct tradition with his sleek and shiny new Luscombe. Barnstorming had died at the time of the expansion of the U.S. Air Mail Service and the creation of the Bureau of Air Commerce in 1926. But Jerry discovered that he could begin paying for his new airplane by barnstorming with it. He began by giving rides to an eager horde of factory employees. Coigny barnstormed locally and along the Atlantic coast for a

Don and Brownee Luscombe pose informally beside Jerry Coigny's Luscombe 50, NC 2591 (serial number 804), shortly before he departed for San Francisco, August 1938.

short while. He also participated in lightplane races sponsored by flying clubs in the area. The Luscombe was quite fast in its class and the prize money added to his earnings. Then, accompanied by Howard Jong, he set off for the west coast. (Jong had gained the valuable experience he had sought at Luscombe and had quit Luscombe to return home to Los Angeles.) Along the way, Coigny and Jong took in the 1938 National Air Races at Cleveland. They flew the little Luscombe in the "Parade of Progress" that opened the races, flying with an Everal propeller provided by Coigny's sponsors.

Coigny's "service reports"

The first service reports on the Luscombe 50 were sent in by Jerry Coigny. He was accumulating more hours, sooner, than anybody. And he was sending a steady stream of letters to West Trenton. After Jerry left West Trenton, he wrote to Lucy regularly. As Jerry was racing and barnstorming in his little Luscombe, much of the news in his letters concerned the performance of his airplane and the problems that the engineers needed to correct. Lucy, the loyal secretary, carefully covered the personal messages with masking tape and showed the letters to higher management.

Fritz King also found out that the Luscombe 50 was a moneymaker. In December he bought serial number 852, partially equipped, for $1000. He borrowed $600 on an insurance policy. Fritz used his own wheels, tailwheel, and instruments and installed them himself, along with some upholstery that the factory had discarded. A snowstorm hit right after he acquired his 50, so he immediately ordered some skis for the plane and became the first to

Fritz King's new 50, December 1938. King's was the first Model 8 to be fitted with skis.

install skis on a Model 8. For a week that airplane never stood still. Everybody wanted to fly King's 50 on skis. Fritz King earned almost enough money in that one week to pay for his airplane.

Luscombe Airplane Company built 71 Model 8s in 1938. Month by month the production rate increased until December, when 21 of them were built.

Don Luscombe and his team had finally come up with a real winner.

5

The war years

Don Luscombe's exciting new product clearly required new manufacturing facilities. The original hangar was too small and too poorly equipped for mass production of the new Model 8. Don badly needed more and better tools, machinery, and factory space. Such additions, however, would require a substantial infusion of new money.

One of the directors learned of a woman broker who had a client—an investment banker—who might be interested in financing the expansion. Vera Montgomery contacted the man, Leopold H.P. Klotz, at his home in Montreal. Klotz was indeed interested.

Klotz personally checked out Don Luscombe and the Luscombe Airplane Company. He was suitably impressed, so he made an initial purchase of the additional stock that the company was issuing.

Although Leopold Klotz was impressed with LAC's potential, it soon became clear that he had reservations about the company's current management and its production practices. Late in the fall of 1938 a Ranger-powered Fairchild 24 landed at Mercer airport. The pilot, Henry Boller, was representing L.H.P. Klotz. He was there to look the plant over.

Business was great at the end of 1938. Production of the Model 8 hit a peak of 21 airplanes in December. Sales of the little two-place continued strong. At the beginning of the year Don moved ahead with his plans to expand the factory. He had his production manager, Ben Melcher, prepare the drawings and the requirements for an addition to the hangar. A contractor was selected and the contracts let in March. Plans also proceeded briskly on the production of the Model 8A.

Late in 1938 Continental was getting ready to produce their 65-hp A-65 engine (ATC #205). Basically the same engine as the A-50, Continental

Chuck Burgess

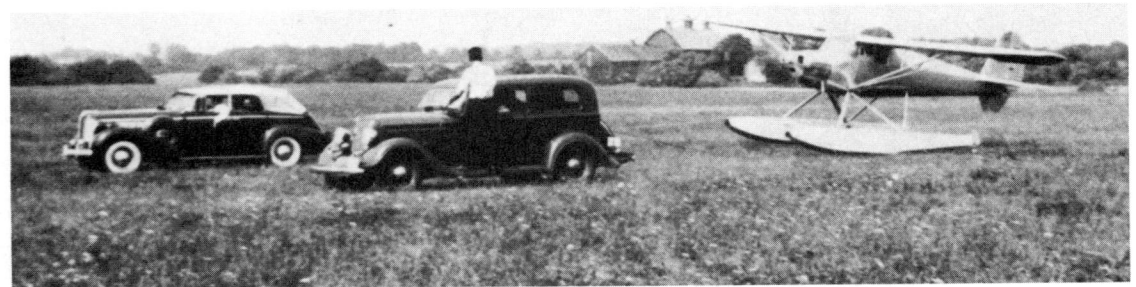

Model 8 seaplane at Mercer Field ready to be towed aloft. The plane was headed for a seaplane dock on nearby Delaware River.

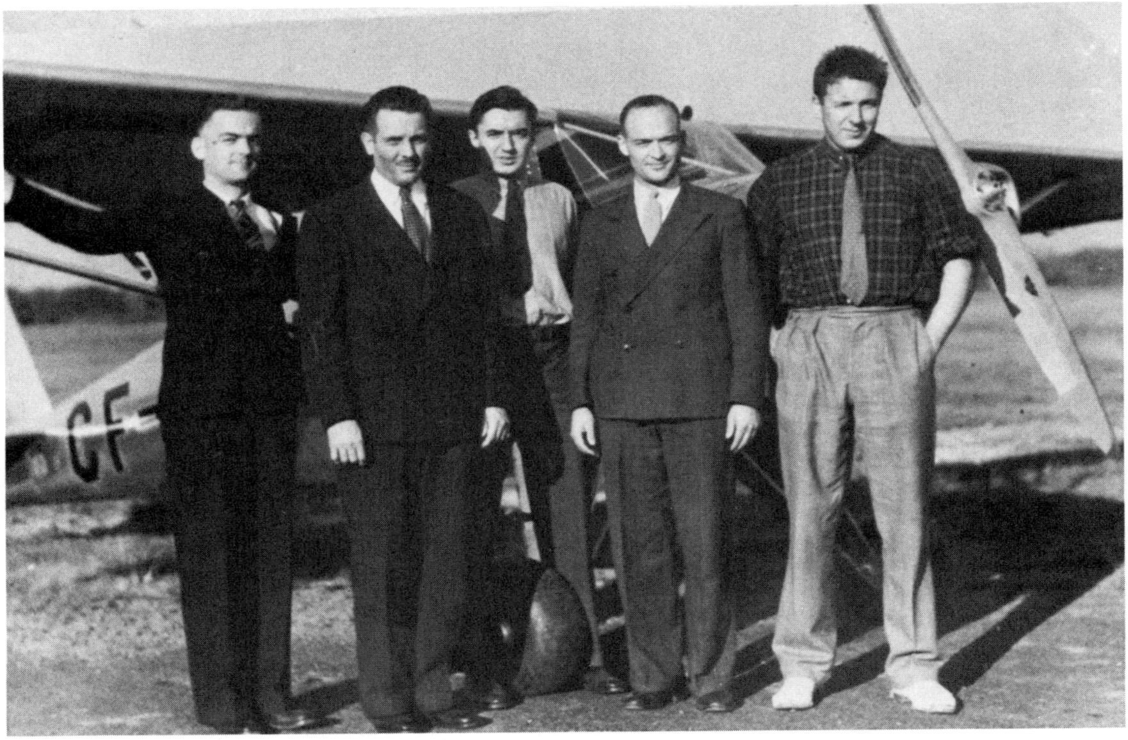

Ig Sargent

Don Luscombe, Eddie Davis (at Don's left), and Ig Sargent with two Canadians. The occasion was delivery of the first 50, CF-BLW, to Canada, fall 1938.

increased takeoff horsepower by raising engine speed to 2300 rpm. An A-65 engine was installed on a Model 8 in January, making the airplane an 8A, and Model 8 production was then rapidly phased out.

Otis Massey, the Luscombe distributor in Denver, took delivery of the last Model 4 (serial number 405) in January 1939. There was no future for the

Factory production of Model 8s.

Model 4, but the Model 8 was going to become the "Tin Lizzie of the Air." Don Luscombe now foresaw a future as bright as the heyday of the Mono-coupes a decade before.

A hostile takeover

Don Luscombe did not realize that a change in fortune of a different sort was in store for him. In January, Henry Boller began to appear regularly at the factory. Boller clearly disliked the way in which the factory was organized and managed. He also took issue with the way many of the employees per-formed their tasks. Affable, slow-talking Ben Melcher, the production man-ager, was under particular scrutiny. In addition to production matters, Mr. Boller also investigated purchasing and sales practices.

Not long afterward, Leopold H.P. Klotz began to flex his muscles. At the February 23 meeting of the board he persuaded the Directors to instruct

Jim Rising hoists a Model-8 fuselage tail cone. It's light and it's strong.

Don Luscombe to hire Henry Boller as production manager. Ben Melcher was removed from the position and assigned full-time to getting the new addition built and equipped for production. Don Luscombe was slipping into a vulnerable position. Leopold Klotz was accumulating Luscombe stock and had become the principal stockholder. Don became concerned about the developing situation. It was conceivable that Klotz and his attorney, Ernst Oberhumer, might soon be able to outvote Don's 18.8 percent of the stock, removing Don as President and Chairman of the Board of Directors. In order to secure his shaky position, Don proposed a contract to the Board of Directors that would retain him as president for another four years.

Crisis in the factory

Resentment flared on the factory floor almost as soon as the new production manager appeared. German-born Henry Boller had a very authoritarian manner. He had strong opinions, was impatient with employees, and worked very poorly with the men under him. He tended toward extremes in both word and deed. It was typical of him to abruptly grab a tool from a worker and show the man the "right" way (the Boller way) to do a job. Henry Boller was like a bull in a china shop.

Henry Boller with Ig Sargent. Don Luscombe was forced to accept Boller as production manager, causing a revolt of the factory workers. The explosive chain of events that followed culminated in the ouster, in April 1939, of Don Luscombe from the company that he founded.

The situation in the factory rapidly escalated to a crisis. One weekend early in March, Don quietly called a meeting of certain key employees in a nearby bar. Don encouraged them to threaten to strike if Klotz didn't remove Henry Boller. The following Monday, March 13, a petition (which Don had written) signed by the key men of the factory was presented to Don. The petition asked for Henry Boller's removal from the position of production manager for the following reasons: (1) Demoralization of factory organization; (2) evident lack of experience with manufacturing; and (3) lack of the quality of leadership and judgment in handling personnel.

Acting on the basis of the petition he himself had instigated, Don Luscombe immediately suspended Henry Boller. He then told Bill Shepard: "You're the production manager now."

Maneuvering during March

As soon as Leopold Klotz learned of Boller's suspension, he contacted Ernst Oberhumer. Klotz's attorney studied the minutes of the February 23 board meeting that had instructed Luscombe to hire Boller as production manager.

He interpreted the terms of employment differently and challenged Don's authority to unilaterally dismiss Henry Boller.

Klotz himself next flew down from his residence in Montreal and began an intensive series of interviews of all parties to the dispute. During the course of these discussions he belittled the efforts and competence of the existing management and implied that unless the men would cooperate with Mr. Boller, he would put no more money into the business. Luscombe Airplane Company would rapidly go broke and leave the men without jobs anyway.

Leopold Klotz also talked at length with Don Luscombe. He informed Don that Ernst Oberhumer (his attorney) had reviewed the law on extended contracts and had concluded that the Board of Directors had no right to contract with Don for such extended services. Klotz further declared his lack of satisfaction with Luscombe's business judgment. He would not only block an extended contract, but he also intended to change the Board of Directors. He held enough proxies to carry out his threat.

On the last day of the month, Don responded by forwarding the employees' petition (requesting that Henry Boller be replaced) to the Board of Directors with a cover letter. In Don's cover letter he pointedly observed that according to U.S. law, a non-citizen could not own *or control* a voting interest of more than 25 percent in a U.S. corporation. (Klotz was an Austrian emigrant and a non-citizen.) Don agreed that legally the stock in Mr. Klotz's name was within the proper limits, but Klotz's recent assumption of details of management seemed to be indicative of his *control*. Don doubted that such control would withstand a federal investigation.

Don Luscombe ousted

The next step in resolving the issue of Henry Boller's retention as production manager took place in New York at the Hotel Lexington. Those attending the meeting were Don Luscombe, George F. Cluett, Jr., Roger Johnson, Ignatius Sargent, Daniel Simonds, and Ernst Oberhumer, proxy for Klotz. Following an extensive discussion of Boller, the board agreed to vote by mail ballots to be postmarked no later than April 5. No one would be hired to replace Boller until after the vote was in and counted.

The meeting was then recessed. When all board members had vacated the room, Oberhumer stated to Don that the present Luscombe management and certain principal stockholders were completely incompatible. Oberhumer then asked Don if he would consider selling his shares in the company and then retire from management. Don Luscombe was licked.

By April 13, 1939, the details of the agreement were finalized for Don to sever his relationship with the company that he had founded. On that same day, Don A. Luscombe resigned from his position as President and member of the Board of Directors of Luscombe Airplane Corporation.

The terms of the sale agreement included Don's resignation as President and Director, along with the resignation of George F. Cluett, Jr., from the board. Don was to sell 16,000 shares at $2.25 per share to Oberhumer, his nominees and assigns. In addition, Don was to receive $7800 in 12 monthly installments of $650 each. He was also to receive a $2000 lump sum payment in compensation for improvements he had made to the Caretaker's House. The agreement further stipulated that Don must not engage in competitive design or manufacture for the period of one year from the date of signing.

It was fitting that Don Luscombe should take one more thing with him from West Trenton. Before he left, Don purchased a shiny new 8A, NC22085 (serial number 907). Leopold Klotz later explained Don's resignation thus: "Having become interested in the development of rotary-winged aircraft, Don A. Luscombe decided to relinquish management of the Luscombe Company to permit full-time activities elsewhere. . . . He resigned in April, 1939, and J.H. Torrens took over as president. . . ."

Exodus

Now the exodus of Luscombe employees began, including the chief engineer, Fred Knack. Pitcairn was starting to build a second fuselage like the one Luscombe had built. Looking out for his own people, Luscombe made arrangements for Pitcairn to take on some of his people with the understanding that he could have these men back when he got back on his feet. Nick Nordyke, who had signed the explosive petition to remove Henry Boller, and Ben Melcher were among those going to Pitcairn.

Bill Shepard and Chuck Burgess, who had also signed the petition, elected to stay with the Luscombe company. Shepard had a limited commercial license, and at the request of the new chief engineer, Jim Rising, Bill began to do test-hopping of the Model 8s coming out of production. Soon the CAA inspector was claiming that Bill's license did not allow him to do that type of flying. By about June, Bill was replaced by Fritz King.

In June, Klotz installed John H. Torrens as president. Torrens promptly named Chuck Burgess to fill the "vacancy" in the position of production manager. Chuck Burgess—not Torrens—informed Bill Shepard of the change. Shepard was livid and immediately confronted Torrens. But Torrens was so uninformed that he hadn't known that Bill Shepard was production manager.

Aerial view of factory shortly after completion of new addition. Factory expansion required a large infusion of new financing. L.H.P. Klotz's investment led to his control of the company, followed by a hostile takeover.

Nevertheless, he stuck by his guns. Shepard, who planned to enroll in graduate school at Purdue in the fall, quit Luscombe and joined his compatriots at Pitcairn for the summer of 1939.

In the midst of the furor, progress continued unabated at the factory. Construction of the factory annex proceeded rapidly and the basic building was completed in June. The following month the assembly line was completed as well. Airplane production also proceeded well. Regular Model 8A production began in April. One 50-hp Model 8 (the last one) was produced in July, at which time 25 Model 8As were produced and the production rate was still climbing.

Model 8A specifications

The addition of 15 more horsepower turned a fine little airplane into a truly great one. The 8A came to be known as the quintessential Luscombe. Its specifications and performance data with the Continental 65-hp (at 2350 rpm) engine, turning a Sensenich wooden propeller, are listed below.

Length, 20 feet 0 inches; height, 5 feet 10 inches; wingspan, 35 feet 0 inches; wing area, 140 square feet; airfoil, NACA 4412.

Weight empty, 665 pounds; useful load, 535 pounds; payload, 273 pounds; gross weight, 1200 pounds; baggage, 55 pounds.

Maximum speed, 115 mph; cruising speed (75 percent power), 102 mph; landing speed, 38 mph; rate of climb, 650 feet per minute.

Cruising range (75 percent power), 370 miles with 14 gallons fuel.

Coigny wedding

Jerry Coigny, who had purchased one of the very first Model 50s, returned to West Trenton in July 1939. He came to accept delivery of a new 65-hp Luscombe 8A. And he came to take home a bride. The story of Jerry Coigny, Lucy Rago, and the "Honeymoon Special" is arguably the most-told story in the lore of the Luscombe.

The French Protestant Jerry Coigny had begun courting the Italian Catholic Lucy Rago the year before. Jerry balked at taking the catechism and converting to Catholicism. The young couple decided to elope. The Coigny 8A, N23035 (serial number 958) became known at the factory as the "Honeymoon Special" and the plane was so marked on the firewall. The other girls at the office helped Lucy smuggle a few personal belongings into the factory, where they were stashed until the proper moment.

On July 12, unbeknownst to Lucy's family, the airplane was loaded with Lucy's belongings and decorated with signs, crepe paper, and old shoes. J.H. Torrens, the new president of the company, gave a farewell speech and presented the couple with a Lear radio. The couple then took off for nearby Doylestown, PA (which required no waiting period), where they were married by a Justice of the Peace. Following the brief ceremony they flew to Wings Field in Ambler, PA. Here the newlyweds spent the night with Don

Lucy Rago and Jerry Coigny seated in Jerry's new 65-hp Luscombe 8A. Shortly thereafter, the couple eloped in this plane. Factory employees "in the know" dubbed it the "Honeymoon Special."

Jerry and Lucy Coigny

and Brownee Luscombe at their newly-purchased Gwynedd Valley estate. The next morning the Coignys bade farewell to the Luscombes and began winging their way west to Grants Pass, OR.

1940

The year 1940 was a somewhat uneventful one at Luscombe. It was, however, a productive one. At year's end the company had almost doubled its production of Model 8s (497) from the year before (257).

One minor event in February was the manufacture of a Phantom, serial number 126. The last Phantom in inventory had been sold late in 1939 and serial number 126 was manufactured from subassemblies manufactured in 1937.

Production manager Chuck Burgess shows off the installation of a Continental A-65 engine in a Luscombe 8A.

The following month, Luscombe began production of the Model 8B. This airplane, a twin of the 8A, was powered by the 65-hp Lycoming O-145-B3 engine (ATC #210). The model was not very popular and sales never came close to those of the Continental-powered 8A.

More propitious was the development of the Model 8C. Management concluded that the time was right to come out with a deluxe model, and Luscombe pulled out all the stops.

An 8A was pulled from the assembly line in April and was modified to become the prototype Model 8C. Engineering installed a 75-hp Continental engine with Excello fuel injectors and dual ignition. The C-75-12 engine (ATC #233), Continental's newest and most powerful, had been redesigned to increase displacement to 188 cubic inches. The airplane was restyled inside and out. The interior finish included upholstery in maroon cloth and tan leather, while the instrument panel, in harmonizing colors, contained a shock-mounted section accented by a chrome band. The control stick was recontoured as well.

The exterior treatment included a restyled cowl that featured grills on the air inlets. The paint scheme included maroon striping on the leading edge of the wing and stripes on the fuselage that streamed back from a prominent letter "S" on the nose. Luscombe-built wheel pants were standard.

Luscombe received CAA approval for the Model 8C on June 17, 1940, and production began the following month. Orders for 8Cs dominated deliveries for the rest of 1940.

The deluxe Luscombe was named the Silvaire and was sold with deluxe advertising. The first full-color Luscombe advertisement appeared in the May 1940 edition of *Aero Digest*.

Aluminum allotments and the Model 8D

As war raged on the European continent in 1940, President Franklin Roosevelt sought to increase the aircraft industry's production capacity to 50,000 airplanes per year. Aluminum to build small commercial airplanes soon became tight. By January of 1941, ERCO could no longer obtain aluminum to build the Ercoupe. The little non-spinnable two-place was unsuitable for pilot training and could not be used in the newly created Civilian Pilot Training Program (CPTP).

The Luscombe, however, was ideally suited for pilot training. In 1940, 74 percent of Luscombe's production was delivered to operators with contracts for the CPTP. Luscombe continued to receive its share of aluminum and on May 28, 1941, the Office of Production Management announced the allotment of aluminum to Luscombe and 10 other lightplane manufacturers:

Aeronca, Howard, Interstate, Meyers, Piper, Porterfield, Rearwin, Stinson, Taylorcraft, and Waco.

Luscombe moved aggressively to increase its share of the market for the Civilian Pilot Training Program and to assure future aluminum allotments. The result was the "Master" 8D. The aircraft they developed used the basic 8A airframe with a new instrument panel equipped with seven holes for instruments so that it could be equipped for instrument flying. The glove compartment was large enough to install the necessary radio equipment. The 8D used the same fuel-injected 75-hp Continental engine as the Silvaire. The 14-gallon fuselage tank in the 8A provided inadequate range. Therefore, it was replaced by two 11½-gallon wing tanks, which provided an advertised range of 550 miles. The bungee trim was replaced by a more modern trim tab on the elevator. The finished design, called the Master, was advertised as being specifically designed and built for the CPTP. The airplane entered production in July as the Model 8D.

The last Phantom

Luscombe management decided to discontinue support of the remaining Phantom fleet in the spring of 1941. This prompted the assembly of the last aircraft. Except for the fuselage, the airplane was assembled from parts on hand. The fuselage that was used to manufacture this airplane was that of the original Phantom, serial number 1, built in Kansas City in 1934. Date of manufacture of the last Phantom was June 17, 1941, and it was licensed as NC28799 (serial number 131). In 1990 this mint-condition Phantom, which was both the first and the last, was flying the airshow circuit in its original colors and original identification number, 272Y.

Luscombe's war effort

America was plunged into the war when the Japanese navy attacked Pearl Harbor on December 7, 1941. The U.S. war effort went into high gear. At the Luscombe Airplane Corporation, J.H. Torrens formed a planning group to develop a plan for the company's war effort. No one yet knew what the government would require of the company, but Luscombe decided to build military aircraft components on contract and not to develop a new aircraft. Production continued on the 8C and 8D airplanes.

A telegram arrived on December 29 requiring the cessation of all civilian production by December 31. The company had on hand or in transit 19 75-hp Continental engines. An inventory of airplane parts indicated that there were parts on hand to assemble an airplane for each of the engines, and the company officials decided to do so. Although the identification plates showed a completion date in January 1942, the weight and balance of each of these aircraft was backdated to December 31, 1941, in order to indicate compliance with the new regulation.

Dick Washburn's sales department now became very active in soliciting new war contracts. When requests for quotes came in, the sales department would send the drawings to production manager Chuck Burgess to make the cost estimates and prepare the quotes.

But suddenly Luscombe seemed unable to win any bids. Smelling a rat, Burgess and Washburn went to Washington. They visited the FBI and could learn nothing. They then went to the Navy's Bureau of Aeronautics and quickly found themselves in conference with a room full of naval officers. The problem with contract awards was worked out, but the two Luscombe representatives were warned that they were not to reveal to anyone anything that had been discussed in that room. If they did so, they would be *shot as spies*. After the sneak attack on Pearl Harbor, the fear of spies and saboteurs was palpable. Burgess and Washburn walked soberly out of the room with sealed lips. They deduced that the problem was that Leopold Klotz, an Austrian citizen, was considered an enemy alien. It was practically a certainty that the U.S. government would take control of the plant.

Almost immediately after the Washington meeting, Luscombe began to obtain contract awards. A contract was signed with Grumman Aircraft early in February to produce tail surfaces for the Grumman F4F Wildcat fighter and bomb bay doors for the TBF Avenger torpedo bomber.

As a result of the investigation of Klotz by the FBI and the U.S. Navy, Klotz's holding company was vested in the Alien Property Custodian Division of the U.S. Treasury Department. On April 7, 1942, the Luscombe company became, in effect, a nationalized industry. The company then reported to Captain Crouse, a former head of the Philadelphia Navy Yard, at the Bureau of Aeronautics. Torrens was demoted to vice president and the Navy brought in Lee Brutus, a former Waco VP, as president. Leopold Klotz moved back to New York and from 1942 until he received his citizenship in 1944, he was associated with a New York investment firm.

During the war years, the Luscombe Aircraft Corporation produced a wide variety of metal products: sheet-metal engine cowlings, bomb bay doors, flaps, ailerons, ammunition feed chutes, ammunition boxes, rudder assemblies, carburetor intake assemblies, metal seats, instrument panels, fuel tanks, ladder assemblies, and a variety of machine parts.

Lee Brutus was eventually replaced by Arthur Hastings as president. Brutus, unhappy with the salary he was making, started a company on the side without the knowledge of the Board of Directors. He placed some of the

Photo on Christmas card (1940) of Luscombe president John H. Torrens. Torrens was president, but L.H.P. Klotz, VP and owner, called the shots.

Luscombe employees in a rented building and began filtering contracts to them. The Navy got wind of the caper and immediately contacted the chairman of the board, Matt Hickey, in Chicago. Lee Brutus was fired and Arthur C. Hastings, Jr., a former Naval officer, was installed in his place.

The Vested Claims Committee eventually determined that Leopold H.P. Klotz was a resident neutral rather than an enemy alien and on June 6, 1944, ruled that the Luscombe holdings should be returned to him. Klotz was granted his U.S. citizenship soon after. He immediately assumed control of the corporation from his position as vice president and treasurer. Upon Hastings' resignation on December 1, 1944, the Board elected Klotz as president.

6

Postwar boom...

As soon as the Allied invasion force had secured a beachhead on France's Normandy coast, it was clear to many that the end of the war in Europe was within reach. Looking forward to a bright postwar future, L.H.P. Klotz soon began the effort to abandon West Trenton and move the Luscombe Company to sunny Texas. Klotz made a trip to Dallas in August 1944 and another in October. Following the second trip, Klotz began negotiations for agricultural land near Garland. One of his requirements was ready access to adequate railroads to bring in shipments of factory material.

The Board of Directors met in early December and Leopold H.P. Klotz was elected president of Luscombe Airplane Corporation, succeeding A.C. Hastings, Jr., who had retired on December 1. The formal decision to move to Dallas was made at that meeting.

Shortly afterwards, Klotz returned to Dallas. Before he left there, he had taken out options to either purchase or lease buildings at 1408 Camp St. in Dallas and had obtained options on about 700 acres of land near Garland.

Klotz returned to Dallas yet again in February 1945. At the conclusion of his two-week trip he had finalized the acquisition of the Garland plant and had made arrangements for immediate construction of a hangar, the first unit in the factory and flying field near Garland. Klotz initially planned to store airplane parts in the hangar until the War Production Board lifted restrictions for light airplane construction. Throughout the effort, the First National Bank of Dallas handled the negotiations for the Luscombe Company. By this time, Klotz had obtained the approval of the War Production Board for the construction and approval of the layout for the factory airfield from the Civil Aeronautics Administration.

Otto Hoernig, Luscombe's operations manager, arrived in Dallas April 3 and was followed shortly by a small contingent of key Luscombe employees

Don Luscombe's four-place design at his Gwynedd Valley, PA home (l. to r.: Don Luscombe, Fred Knack, and Ben Melcher). The plane, mothballed during WWII, was designed by Fred Knack and Edgar Mitchell; built by a few of Don's loyal long-time employees.

Luscombe sold plane and plans to Raymond Weatherly and William Campbell of Dallas, TX, in May 1946. The gull-winged four-place (190-hp Lycoming O-435-A) was named the Colt. Weatherly-Campbell abandoned the project after losing a 1948 bid for a four-place Army liaison aircraft.

from the West Trenton operation, including Fred Knack, engineering vice-president, and James Cunningham, factory superintendent. Local workers were recruited and trained through April and May. By June 1, contracts had been negotiated for the 100-foot-wide and 600-foot-long main assembly building, experimental hangar, and T-hangars to be built on the Garland premises.

The Luscombe business plan was based on producing an 85-hp Continental version of the 1941 Model 8D. Luscombe's first postwar magazine advertisement was a full-page, full-color announcement featuring a 1941 Model 8C, which appeared in the January issue of *Southern Flight*. Later, advertisements in the May through June issues of the same magazine were geared toward dealership recruitment and included coupons that prospective dealers could return to the factory.

Stamped-rib wing assembly, May 1946.

Imitation, the sincerest form of flattery

Other aircraft manufacturers were also tooling up to take advantage of the postwar boom in general aviation aircraft that was being forecast.

The most promising market appeared to be the one for a two-place airplane for flight training and private ownership. Early in 1945, Cessna made the decision to enter that market. Cessna studied the competition thoroughly before deciding upon the configuration of their entry. They owned several prewar lightplanes: an Ercoupe, a 1941 Luscombe 8C (NC 41914, serial number 1875), a Piper Family Cruiser, and a Stinson 10 (three-seat, with 90-hp Lycoming engine). Cessna officials decided to adopt the configuration represented by the Luscombe 8. At the time, Cessna's engineers were working on the "Family Car of the Air," a fabric-covered fuselage prototype of the Model 190/195 series (an upgrade of their popular prewar Airmaster). Following the decision to build a two-place, the engineering effort was concentrated on its design and construction.

Cessna's engineers dissected the Luscombe and then went on to design their version. They installed Cessna-style wings of a lower aspect ratio; these incorporated landing flaps. Cessna's engineers widened the cabin slightly, deleted the cabane struts, and installed the increasingly popular wheel control. They also incorporated the spring-steel landing gear invented by race pilot Steve Wittman and installed hydraulically-actuated toe brakes. The Cessna 140 was powered by Continental's latest entry to the engine market, the 85-hp C-85-12 engine. The lines of the basic airframe and the corrugated aluminum control surfaces left no doubt as to the design's ancestry. The Cessna 140 prototype first took to the air on June 28, 1945.

Model 8 production: Let's get moving!

In Dallas that same month, Luscombe engineers discussed whether to update the Silvaire line or replace it with a new aircraft. Numerous engineering changes were proposed for the Model 8, and the West Trenton advertising department suggested changing to a Model 9 for all postwar aircraft. The proposal for model change was submitted to the CAA. The suggestion died when the CAA pointed out that a model change would require complete recertification, while engineering updates could be approved without recertification.

By mid-September, all of the Luscombe company's civilian aircraft manufacturing had been moved to Dallas. Tooling for the Phantom and the Model 4 was abandoned at West Trenton.

The first Dallas-built aircraft, an 8D, was completed on August 12. Three more 8Ds were completed in September, at which time Luscombe com-

Factory employees posed on the wing of a Model 8 became a Luscombe publicity cliché. The airplane in this May 1946 photo is a new 8A built with a stamped-rib wing.

pleted its last World War II military contract and was presented with the coveted Army-Navy E Award.

Gene Norris, chief engineer

Late in the summer the chief engineer, Fred Knack, turned in his resignation to Klotz. Klotz turned to E.W. "Gene" Norris for help. Klotz was well acquainted with Norris, who was Technical Director of the Aircraft Industries Association (AIA). Additionally, Norris was a private pilot and a graduate of the Guggenheim School of Aeronautics and New York University.

Klotz respected Norris highly and had made an earlier attempt to lure him to Luscombe. "Fred Knack walked out on me," Leopold told Gene. "Will you come to Luscombe as my chief engineer?" This time Norris said yes. He visited the Luscombe plant in October to assess the situation. He began work the first of November with the intention of building a solid engineering department for Klotz and staying about a year.

Edgar Mitchell acted as chief engineer during the interval between the Knack departure and the Norris arrival. During this time the engineering and the tooling departments were doing their utmost to increase the production rate. During the months of September through November, the tooling department completely updated or replaced all Luscombe assembly tooling.

View of engineering department. Gene Norris, chief engineer (l. foreground), chats with Doug Clements while Merle Mueller listens in. The balding individual leaning over the drafting table (l. rear) is engineering illustrator Hi Walker. Note model of Norris' four-place pusher suspended over his head.

The prewar assembly jigs were inadequate for the volume production anticipated from the Dallas plant.

The insignificant increase in production to only six 8Ds in October was very disappointing and Klotz decided instead to gear the operation toward producing the 65-hp 8A. An initial order for 500 Continental A-65 engines was placed at the same time.

On October 25, Luscombe's production plans were set back when a fire destroyed nearly all of the airplane seat cushions and padding at the downtown plant. The rate at which production increased remained agonizingly slow. Only 38 8As were completed in December. As the majority of the 55 8As and 11 8Ds produced in 1945 were in the dealer/distributor pipeline, very few Luscombe aircraft reached customers by year's end.

Under Mitchell's leadership, the engineers mounted their assault upon the production problem early. During the summer the engineering department launched an effort that was to extend throughout the following year of 1946. The goal was to redesign the details and assemblies to make the airplane as simple and inexpensive to build as possible.

The first of the major production changes was incorporated when the new production tooling was completed during the third week of December. In all previous Model 8s, fuselage stations three through seven were assembled as one unit. Starting with serial number 1975, fuselage stations three and four were assembled in one jig, five through seven in a separate jig. The two assemblies where then joined farther down the assembly line. The fuselage splice strip was shortened and reached from stations four to seven. Not long before that, at serial number 1934, a one-piece upper and lower fuselage tail cone skin replaced the four-piece skin used previously. At the same time, the firewall was changed to utilize an aluminum stamping.

Stamped-rib wings

The next engineering project was to simplify construction of the wing. The multi-piece, built-up ribs were abandoned. The replacements were simple stamped metal ribs that were designed to be quickly slipped over the spars and easily riveted in place. The rib spacing was revised between the wing root and the aileron, with the result that the stamped-rib version had 14 ribs compared to 13 on the original wing and used slightly longer struts.

Norris began the effort to strengthen the engineering department almost as soon as he arrived. He soon augmented the residual nucleus of young engineers from Trenton with several carefully selected aero engineering graduates from the University of Texas and from Texas A&M (most with wartime Army Aviation, Navy, or USAF flying experience), and with two experienced engineers from Beech—Herbert Kueck (design) and H.G. "Gus" Erickson (structures). Norris knew Herb Kueck of Beechcraft through his AIA activities. Kueck had contributed significantly to the design of the new Beech Bonanza. He was more than willing to join Luscombe as assistant chief engineer. Kueck, in turn, recruited fellow Beech engineer Gus Erickson to add depth to Luscombe engineering's stress analysis capabilities. Kueck arrived early in January 1946; Erickson early the following month.

Decision for an all-metal wing

Shortly after Norris arrived he initiated a research project to lighten and simplify the nose ribs. He next began to explore the structural requirements for a stressed-skin, all-metal wing. Norris then had his experimental shop construct assemblies to investigate the strength of metal skins stiffened with T-sections. The research paid off far sooner than he expected.

During a staff meeting early in January, Leopold Klotz described the problems of obtaining both aircraft fabric and the steel bracing wire used to manufacture the wing. These shortages would soon limit the rate of wing production. Norris observed that *both* problems would be eliminated if Luscombe went to a stressed-skin, all-metal wing, using the existing extruded spars. The results of engineering's investigations in the experimental shop were showing great promise.

"Can you do that?"

"All we need is your go-ahead."

"Do it, do it," exclaimed Klotz.

Gene Norris put the metal wing project on the front burner and when Gus Erickson arrived the following month, he was assigned as project engineer.

Model 10

A few days before the all-metal wing decision (during the first week in January), there occurred another event of less enduring significance. The single-place Luscombe Model 10 flew for the first time. Four months before that, in the first week of September 1945, Mischa Kantor, an acquaintance of Klotz's, convinced the president that a low-wing, single-place aircraft using a significant number of Model 8 parts had merit. Kantor asserted that with a crew of three men, he could assemble an airplane separately from the engineering department. Kantor's project was designated Model 10.

The airplane was built quickly from sketches by seat-of-the-pants engineering with no structural analysis. Wing area for the single-place was reduced by shortening the wing spars, which were simply bolted together to obtain the desired dihedral. Fin and rudder area was reduced by the simple expedient of removing the top portion of the production assembly. The stabilizer and elevator were standard 8A parts as well as everything from the firewall forward. A fuselage center section, including canopy and landing gear, were formed by hand in the experimental hangar.

The Model 10 prototype was completed by the end of November. Flight tests were delayed while all personnel participated in the big push to get 8A production under way.

In the last week of December, Bob Burns taxied out for the Model 10's first flight. The landing gear began to wobble badly and the taxi tests were abandoned before the landing gear collapsed. The airplane was pushed back

Single-place Model 10 (65-hp Continental) designed by Mischa Kantor is shown in flight during its short-lived flight test career.

into the experimental hangar, where the wing center section was beefed up and the landing gear was attached more securely.

Following the structural repair of the landing gear, Burns conducted the maiden flight the first week of January. Later, in the March issue of *Skyways*, Burns is reported to have said: "You've got a good airplane just like it is. Don't change a thing."

The company undertook a survey to assess the size of the market. If there was such a market, the Model 10's likely competition would be Piper's Skycycle and Lockheed's Little Dipper designed by John Thorp. The survey indicated, however, that the market was too small. The Model 10 was never produced and ultimately the prototype met an inglorious end in a windstorm.

As soon as the Model 10 entered flight test, Kantor immediately assembled a four-man crew and began construction of a two-place, side-by-side, low-wing aircraft. However, the project was very short-lived. During the last week of January, the engineering department revolted. In a meeting with Klotz, they pointed out that Kantor's aircraft were not marketable without sufficient data to certify and produce the aircraft. To avoid costly mistakes, information should come from their department first. They also reminded him that with production running behind schedule, the four-man crew was needed on the assembly line. Klotz agreed, the project was scrapped, and Mischa Kantor and his experimental team returned to the assembly line.

All-metal wing design

As soon as Gus Erickson arrived at Luscombe, he dived into the all-metal wing project. He began methodically. Seeking to design the least expensive metal wing, he instructed the engineers on the team to conduct time studies of existing assemblies to determine which types of construction operations to avoid and which to favor. Welding, machining, holding close tolerances, and driving rivets by hand proved to be expensive operations. Brakes and punch presses were the cheapest way to form parts, and driving rivets automatically was the cheapest way to attach parts.

The design used preformed skin sections, reinforced with hat sections riveted to the spars. (The hat sections were cheaper, lighter, and stronger than the T sections used on the test panels.) Ribs were eliminated! The end result was a wing consisting of a metal shell structure built around two metal

This view of a metal wing, shown here in fabrication fixture, illustrates stark simplicity of the design.

spars and two ribs. In simplifying the fabrication, the designers paid particular attention to the number of operations necessary to complete each part. Different right- and left-hand parts were eliminated wherever possible. All rivet spacings were designed to a maximum consistent with strength requirements.

In the production method finally adopted, the six main skin panels, two trailing edge panels, and two nose sections—all of which were structurally complete in themselves—were riveted up as subassemblies. Extensive use was made of the automatic riveter, and hand-driven rivets were used only to attach the subassemblies to the two extruded spars. No bolts were used anywhere in the entire wing panel assembly.

Total cost and weight were further reduced by a use of a single lift strut, which was extruded from aluminum alloy to a hollow, streamlined shape with stamped steel fittings riveted in each end. This single strut replaced the old arrangement of two lift struts and three jury struts, all of which were of steel and required welding, machining, and the holding of closer tolerances.

A nonflying mockup was constructed and after some minor refinements, the experimental shop produced two all-metal wings. These were installed on an aircraft from the assembly line in early April and flight testing began immediately. Norris and Erickson flew the prototype to Kansas City for CAA flutter tests, which were successfully conducted on April 18.

Then a severe rainstorm swept the factory area in mid-May and a small twister destroyed 12 completed aircraft, including the first metal-wing prototype (NX45869). A second set of wings had been built for structural test;

Original fin structure drawn by engineering illustrator "Hi" Walker. The original version consisted of 13 parts: 2 spars, 4 ribs, 5 skins, 1 cast attach fitting, and 1 splice/attach fitting. Top skin pieces required two separate dies. The fin required 3¼ man-hours to assemble.

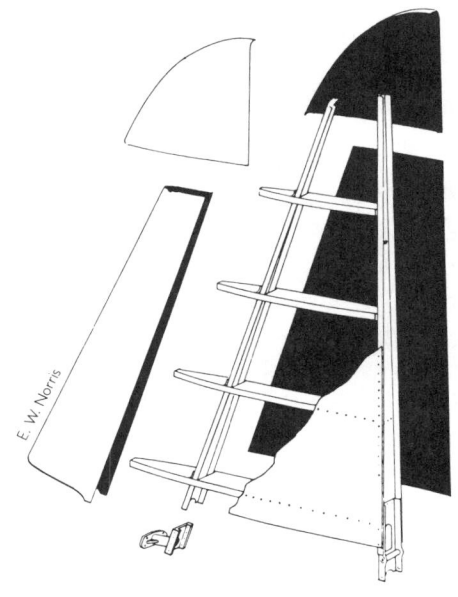

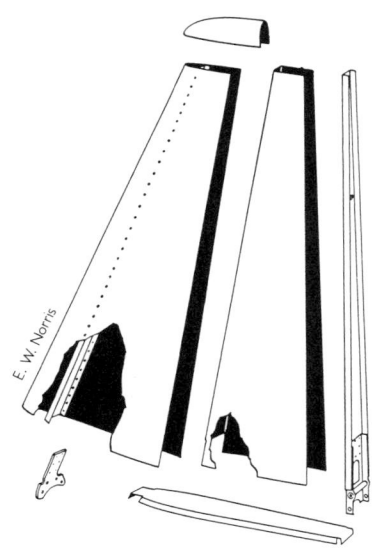

Simplified square fin, introduced into production April 1947, exemplifies engineering's several achievements in developing cheaper, simpler assemblies. This improved version consisted of only 8 parts: 2 spars, 1 rib, 2 skins, 1 fin-tip fairing, and 2 attach fittings. The fairing began as one canoe-shaped part that was cut in half to make two identical parts. The new fin required only 1 1/2 man-hours to assemble.

now the experimental shop produced a third set of preproduction wings and the week of May 19, serial number 2727 (NX71300) was mated with the new metal wings and the first flight-test program continued.

Production competition

Despite the valiant effort made to increase production, Luscombe delivered only 210 aircraft in May 1946. Aeronca and Cessna production rates were not made public for May, but Piper produced 733 aircraft and Taylorcraft 550. ERCO could produce 10 Ercoupes per shift on their highly automated production line. ERCO was operating two full shifts per day and produced 455 aircraft. With a backlog of 1000 orders on file, Luscombe's nine-per-day production rate was unacceptable.

The two-place pusher

Ever since the move to Dallas, engineering had been discussing a two-place pusher as a replacement for the Model 8. Klotz now drastically revised the timetable for the pusher project. At his staff meeting on Monday, June 3, 1946, Klotz told his staff—the heads of the engineering, sales, and production departments—of his decision to produce a four-place aircraft (which was to become the Model 11). At this time the executives decided that the available engineering time at Luscombe would be divided between a continuing improvement program on the current two-place series and the design of a four-place aircraft, rather than the development of a completely new two-place pusher design.

During the latter stages of the war, aeronautical engineers began to think of new airplane designs for general aviation in the postwar world. There was a groundswell of interest in pusher designs. All efforts to produce such an airplane eventually came to naught, but Lockheed and Douglas built prototypes of the Big Dipper and the Cloudster, respectively, while Anderson-Greenwood went into limited production of the AG-14. (Ironically, Frank Johnson, whose 1937 design studies initiated the Luscombe Model 8, was severely injured on a takeoff crash of Lockheed's Big Dipper prototype.)

There was keen pusher interest within the Luscombe engineering department as well. The Dallas engineering department favored replacing the Model 8 with a two-place pusher aircraft.

Early in the Dallas operation, Klotz agreed with engineering's suggestion to purchase an existing pusher aircraft for trial purposes. The only one available at the time was a 1939 Stearman-Hammond. The all-metal Model Y1S would give the engineering department a flying example. While test pilot Bob Burns was ferrying an out-of-license Stearman-Hammond, the engine quit. He made a deadstick landing, during which the outer wing panels were damaged. The panels were never repaired, but engineering conducted several high-speed taxi tests to evaluate the novel tricycle landing gear.

Before Gene Norris had come to Luscombe, he had done some preliminary design for a twin-propeller, four-place pusher and had had a model made of it. Norris accepted the position of chief engineer at Luscombe with the hope that he would be able to design and develop a Luscombe all-metal pusher aircraft. He soon realized that Luscombe had neither the facilities nor the personnel to accomplish such a daunting task anytime soon. Nevertheless, a model of his pusher hung above his desk throughout the time that he remained at Luscombe.

Herb Kueck, who had worked at Beech Aircraft through the war and had been a member of the Bonanza design team, had also developed a pusher design of his own. As time permitted, the engineering department continued pusher research with the goal of eventually replacing the Model 8 series. The engineering emphasis was soon placed on Herb Kueck's high-wing, twin-boom airplane.

Klotz's decision in June had not killed the pusher concept; it only had delayed implementation. The pusher concept raised its head one last time at the distributors' meeting in October. The engineering department completed a scale model and was granted time at that meeting to make a presentation. The engineering presentation and the pusher model (designated the Luscombe Model 12) received an enthusiastic reception from the distributors. Then the distributors wanted to know how quickly the design team

Leopold H. P. Klotz (left) in front of the 500th Silvaire in Dallas, April 1946.

could get their airplane to the customer. They were told that the development program would take 14 to 18 months. Since deliveries of the pusher could not be started in the first quarter of 1947, they lost interest. Emphasis at the meeting quickly changed to the improvement and selling of conventional airplanes, and Luscombe management soon ordered the pusher design scrapped.

8E introduced

The maroon-and-silver, 85-hp Luscombe 8E, billed as the "140 killer," was introduced to the distributors at that same meeting. The latest model first appeared in June, when the experimental shop converted a rag-wing 8A. The 8E, which received CAA approval in June, featured back windows, a hat-throw, and two 12½-gallon wing tanks in lieu of a single fuselage tank.

Aerial view of Luscombe plant looking southeast in August 1946, right at company's peak. Farmhouse in upper left was occupied by design team working on Model 11 Sedan.

The distributors ordered slightly more than 800 8Es before the end of the three-day meeting. But they were keenly aware that the lightplane boom had already passed.

A reckoning

The year 1946 ended with Luscombe far behind the leaders in the production race. Piper, Aeronca, and Cessna were America's top lightplane producers during 1946, according to an Aircraft Industries Association tabulation. This same yearly summary showed companies delivered 31,187 lightplanes worth $88,172,000. The 14 firms were ranked as follows by units manufactured: 1) Piper, 7780; 2) Aeronca, 7555; 3) Cessna, 3559; 4) Taylorcraft, 3151; 5) Ercoupe, 2503; 6) Luscombe, 2483; 7) Stinson, 1436; 8) Globe Swift, 1054; 9) Temco (Globe Swift & Fairchild contractor), 563; 10) Beech, 299; 11) Bellanca, 288; 12) Republic, 196; 13) Funk, 174; and 14) North American, 146.

7

... and bust

During the months immediately following Gene Norris' arrival at Luscombe, the engineering department's efforts were directed toward developments to facilitate production, reduce costs, and generally to improve the Model 8 series. But it soon became apparent that Luscombe also needed a four-place entry to the lightplane market. And they needed it *now*.

At about this time, the Flying Farmers Association (FFA) released specifications for its ideal farm/ranch airplane. The specs called for rugged simplicity, off-airport operational capability, a large-volume cabin for multipurpose use, comfort, good cabin visibility, and low cost. The company's marketing information indicated that 80 percent of all Luscombes being sold were going into rural areas. Thus, it seemed that the FFA represented one of the largest potential customer groups for four-place airplanes.

On Monday, June 3, 1946, at his staff meeting with the heads of the engineering, sales, and production departments, Klotz announced his decision to produce a four-place aircraft. At this time, the executives decided that the available engineering time at Luscombe would be divided between a continuing improvement program on the current two-place series and the design of the four-place aircraft, rather than the development of a completely new two-place pusher design. Klotz stated that Herb Kueck would be the project engineer.

With full company support of the design objectives, Herb and his preliminary design team were isolated in a farmhouse in mid-field and directed to develop a design that would meet the FFA specs and make full use of the simplified design and manufacturing concepts that had recently been incorporated in the Model 8 series. The four-place was designated as the Model 11.

Engineers assigned to the Sedan design team worked separately in a farmhouse located on the field. Seen here are (l. to r.): Roy Ockles, Doyle Brooks, Roy Moses, Herb Kueck (project engineer), Les Kristjen, Bob Burns, Roy Chumley, and Gus Erickson.

The concept of a four-place pusher still had strong adherents within engineering, but given the design requirements, the internal debate was quickly resolved in favor of a "conventional" configuration.

Wing design

The designers decided immediately that the airplane should be a high-wing model. For farmers and ranchers, downward visibility is of particular importance, and for cargo-carrying, it was deemed necessary that cargo loading be rapid and simple. The high wing offered the additional advantages of greater flight stability, and allowed the use of a gravity fuel system, the most dependable and trouble-free type known. Fuel system reliability was further enhanced by the decision to equip the engine with a common float-type carburetor.

The FFA four-place was intended to operate from short, unimproved airfields and take off over high mesquite. Thus, a high aspect ratio wing was chosen because of the excellent results achieved with the Model 8 and the advantages such a wing offered in the way of short takeoff and fast climb.

The NACA 4412 airfoil used on the Model 8 was also well-suited for the four-place application. Similarly, a 165-hp engine was selected to provide a good margin of power for operations from unimproved fields.

Flaps were omitted on the original prototype since they complicated the manufacture and operation of the airplane. However, flight testing later demonstrated that flaps would be necessary as a glide-control device. The combination of high aspect ratio, high optimum lift, and relatively low wing loading resulted in a flat glidepath that was unacceptable for short-field operation.

The large flaps that were subsequently added to the design had hinge moments that were too large to handle conveniently with a direct manual operating system. The designers finally developed a simple, one-line hydraulic system that operated satisfactorily. A double-acting hand pump, convenient to both pilots' positions, required about five strokes to extend the flaps fully. A release valve, operated by a trigger on the pump handle, served to raise the flaps. Both the flaps were operated from one actuating cylinder.

The intended use of the airplane dictated that it be equipped with a fixed conventional-type landing gear. The landing gear was longer than usual so that the airplane could operate from rough fields. One consequence was that on the ground the rear seat passengers sat at a rather uncomfortable

Horace Scoggins, Luscombe's chief test pilot, pauses beside the first production model of the Silvaire Sedan following successful completion of production flight tests.

angle. The 100-inch width of the landing gear made the plane stable on the ground and virtually eliminated the possibility of ground-looping.

Cabin design

The finished cabin design clearly met the requirements of a roomy cabin for multipurpose use with good visibility. The rear seat was of the hammock type and was easily removed by taking out the front and rear support tubes. This provided an unobstructed cargo floor approximately 3.5 feet square, providing room to carry six milk cans. The right-hand front seat could also be removed to provide additional cargo space. The floor was made of heavy gauge material, suitably supported by heavy floor beams. It featured anchorage points and five tiedown straps. Access was provided by a large door on each side, with a floor-level sill.

Ron Price

NC 1606B in flight.

Spacious cockpit of Luscombe Model 11A Sedan.

The farmer/rancher/pilot could certainly see out. The Silvaire Sedan had approximately 3716 square inches of window area, "giving it a visibility equal to that of most popularly priced automobiles." There was also an unusual degree of downward visibility over the nose.

The unpainted bare-bones prototype took to the air on schedule and with little fanfare early in November 1946.

Tandem 8E

In the spring of 1947, the Air Force announced that it would purchase approximately 400 off-the-shelf lightplanes for liaison use by the Army ground forces. The bid proposal called for an 85-hp, high-wing, tandem aircraft. The Air Force proposal required an aircraft that was either in current production or held a current type certificate. The Model 8E was certificated and the engineering department was convinced that it would be relatively easy to convert an 8E to tandem configuration. Gene Norris assigned Merle Mueller to be the project engineer on the effort. For a brief, intense period, all engineering effort was directed toward developing an aircraft to win the off-the-shelf bid. Even the 11A team was diverted for approximately three weeks.

An 8E was diverted from the production line and modified with as few changes as possible. The prototype XT-8E used 90 percent of the 8E's parts. Luscombe's entry to the competition was trucked to Fort Bragg, SC, where the Air Force conducted all evaluations of Army aircraft. (At that time the Army had neither the authority nor the capability to evaluate airplanes.) All entrants—Aeronca, Luscombe, and Taylorcraft—successfully completed the flight evaluation phase. Aeronca won the competition with a remarkably low bid of $1649 per airplane and signed a contract for delivery of 439 Model 7BCs—far below the price that Leopold Klotz needed to build the T8E.

After the unsuccessful military bid, the Model T8E was crated and shipped back to Dallas. Assigned number NX2788K, flight testing continued so the CAA certification could be obtained. By this time, Luscombe already had a considerable sum invested in the tandem aircraft and believed that the government would make additional off-the-shelf buys in subsequent years.

Merle Mueller

Original prototype of XT-8E. Compared to the production version, this one had a small bubble and a flat skylight.

Silflex gear

The major efforts on the Model 8 manufacturing simplification, on developing the Model 11 Sedan, and on the T8E Tandem were complete by mid-1947. Gene Norris now had the time and resources to address the Model 8's landing gear problem.

The parts department was doing a good business—*too* good, thought Norris—supplying landing gear parts to flying schools and private owners who had broken their landing gear in ground-loop accidents. Norris determined to design a more robust gear that was less prone to ground-loop. He assigned his top designer, Herb Kueck, as project engineer.

Kueck studied the deficiencies of the Model 8's existing gear as well as the advantages claimed by Cessna for their cantilever spring-steel landing gear. Then he set to work. Kueck concluded that the spring-steel gear primarily relied upon side friction of the tires against the ground for its snubbing action. That contributed to tire wear. By contrast, he designed a cantilever tubular-steel gear attached to a combination coil-spring/oleo unit. The resulting Silvaire flexible gear, called "Silflex," offered the simplicity of a spring-type gear with the light weight and shock absorption of an oleo gear—and the tread was four inches wider.

First production of Silflex landing gear.

The primary improvements of the new design included: installing a sturdier, heat-treated chrome-molybdenum alloy, tubular-steel leg featuring a step taper from 2³/4 inches at the top to 1¹/2 inches at the bottom, redesigning the hydraulic unit with a piston head that gave better control of oil flow and improved uniform shock absorption, and installing the latest O-ring type packing to replace the original Chevron-type packing.

The new Silflex gear was easier to produce; a steel forging was substituted for the original built-up welded structure, tubing with a close tolerance inside diameter was used to fabricate the hydraulic cylinder, and the new gear used 17 percent fewer parts.

Gene Norris himself conducted some of the engineering evaluation of the new Silflex gear. Later, he delighted in demonstrating the obviously superior, ground-loop resistant gear to visiting distributors and other buyers.

Model 11 spin problem

The Luscombe Sedan had been designed for the flying farmer/rancher. Appropriately, one of the prototypes, N2727K, was flown to the National Flying Farmers Association meeting at Oklahoma A & M in August 1947. The Model 11 was the sensation of the fly-in.

Luscombe introduced the Sedan to the larger public at the Texas State Fair in October, but the Sedan program received a serious setback in December 1947. Engineer/pilot Frank Chapman was conducting a series of spin tests for certification. He started the series with a relatively light load and with forward CG and worked back gradually to the condition of maximum gross weight and rear CG. On December 2, Chapman was performing spins at design gross weight with the airplane loaded at 37 percent MAC (mean aerodynamic chord), the rear limit. Starting at 8,000 feet altitude, he recovered from a 1¹/2-turn left spin. He next attempted a 2¹/2-turn left spin, but before he completed the second turn, the spin became uncontrollable. The nose rose and the spin became definitely flat, then the engine began smoking badly and losing power and soon quit. Chapman hit the silk at 3500 feet. NX2727K, *sans* pilot, impacted in a flat spin.

The engineering department finally settled on two fixes that would both satisfy the CAA certification requirements and require the least modification to the design. First, the center of gravity envelope was narrowed to limit the permissible amount of rear loading. Then, the up-elevator travel was limited to 13 degrees, which made it virtually impossible to stall the aircraft while operating under normal flight conditions. The Model 11A became a nearly spinproof aircraft. The negative side effect was that there was insufficient elevator travel to make a conventional landing; the Sedan was limited to wheel landings only. This restriction was *not* a selling point with many of the airplane's potential customers.

Luscombe management now discovered from their distributors that the flying farmer market, for which the Sedan was designed, was nonexistent. The Sedan's actual market would be mostly businessmen. The idea of hauling milk cans with the Sedan was abandoned. Instead, the interior of the 1948 Sedan used pin-striped wool upholstery, automobile-type carpeting, ashtrays, and a dome light purchased from the Cadillac Division of General Motors. Thus equipped, the Luscombe Model 11A was certified by the CAA on May 18, 1948.

Model 11A Sedan specifications

The Model 11A Silvaire Sedan, powered with the 165-hp (at 2050 rpm) Continental E-165 engine, was offered to the flying public advertising the following specifications and performance:

Length, 23 feet 6 inches; height, 6 feet 10 inches; wingspan, 38 feet 0 inches; total wing area, 165 square feet; airfoil, NACA 4412.

Weight empty, 1280 pounds; useful load, 1000 pounds; payload, 571 pounds; baggage, 100 pounds; gross weight, 2280 pounds.

Maximum speed, 140 mph plus; cruising speed (at 74 percent power), 130 mph; landing speed (with flaps), 55 mph; takeoff run, 800 feet; climb, 900 feet first minute from sea level; service ceiling, 17,000 feet; cruising range (at 1850 rpm), 500 miles.

Gas capacity, 42 gallons; oil capacity, 10 quarts.

Price at the factory, $6995.

Tough times

Only days after rollout of the first Silflex landing gear in January, the first production Model 8F, incorporating a 90-hp Continental engine, was also rolled out of the factory. The company then followed suit with the tandem aircraft and the powerplant certification programs were conducted simultaneously for the 8F and the T8F. Approval for both aircraft arrived from the CAA on March 22, 1948.

But the improvements in the products were incapable of bolstering sagging sales. The first break in the postwar boom in lightplane sales had occurred in the fall of 1946. Twice in 1947—two weeks in January and another two weeks in late June and early July—Luscombe had shut down the production line to allow deliveries to catch up with production. Lagging sales and the heavy expenses of developing the Sedan continued to take their toll. Leopold Klotz could no longer afford the services of his highest-paid managers. Effective

February 1, the following executives resigned: James P. Cunningham, vice president in charge of production; James J. Brophy, secretary-treasurer; and James L. Camp, sales promotion director. Otto W. Hoernig, assistant to the president in charge of sales and service, was elected to the Luscombe Board of Directors. Later that spring Gene Norris, vice president of engineering, and Herb Kueck, chief engineer, also resigned from the engineering department. Effective April 15, H.G. Erickson was appointed chief engineer.

During the course of 1948, Luscombe launched several special efforts to keep the company afloat: the "Silvairizing" program, the "Sky Pal" program, the "Crop Master" program, and the effort with the Sedan to break the continuous flight record for a lightplane.

The "Silvairizing" program, introduced in March, permitted the owner of any flyable "stick-and-rag" airplane powered by a 65-hp Continental engine to have that airplane "converted" into a modern, all-metal Luscombe Silvaire. The perfectly good engine, wheels, tires, tailwheel, and flight instruments would be removed from the obsolete airplane and used on the new Silvaire. The certificate of the old airplane would be surrendered to the CAA and the airplane would be withdrawn permanently from service so that it would no longer depress used airplane values. The "Silvairized" airplane that took its place would in every sense be a *new* Silvaire except that instead of using expensive items of purchased equipment (engine, etc.), it used those already owned by the owner or operator.

The Silvaire Sky Pal was offered to reach a larger number of low-budget pilots. This was a bare-bones 8A that retailed for only $2095. (By comparison, the Deluxe T8F, with starter and landing lights, retailed at $3195.)

One other effort was made to reach a new market with a minimum of development cost. Luscombe management decided to develop the T8F as a crop sprayer. Management felt that new model development was essential to the survival of the company, but lacking funds to develop a new aircraft, they had to utilize the existing line to its fullest. In November, Klotz announced that the T8F sprayer would be called the "Crop Master." Developed as a farm implement, it would be certified and ready for delivery at the start of the spring spraying season.

Finally, Klotz and his staff decided to improve the Sedan's image by trying to break the continuous flight record for a lightplane. In 1948, this record stood at 726 hours (30+ days). Sedan NX1601B (serial number 11-111) was modified for the flight and christened *Miss Texas*. Luscombe's goal was 60 days. The record attempt was made in October by two Dallas ex-Air Force pilots, Fred Vinmont and Bert Simon, sponsored by the Texas Private Fliers Association (TPFA). The pilots refueled in flight by snatching five-gallon cans of fuel with a grappling hook from a Ford convertible racing down the runway of Dallas' Love Field.

The attempt fared about the same as Klotz's other endeavors in 1948. The endurance record flight ended 529 hours (22 days) after takeoff when the engine suddenly quit and NX1601B crash-landed at night in a small clearing in a wooded area near Long View, TX.

The heroic efforts of 1948 were all to no avail. Beginning December 1, many suppliers—including Continental Motors—put Luscombe Airplane Corporation on a COD basis. The company had begun to build Sedans in batches of 10. After they lost the ability to float checks and stretch out the payment of invoices, the factory completed only eight Sedans of the last batch.

Bankruptcy

Luscombe cash-flow problems had been severe since the first of the year. By November, Klotz was attempting to negotiate reconstruction finance loans from the Reconstruction Finance Agency. He was unsuccessful, and by March 1949 he was unable to meet the payroll. The employees were persuaded to accept half pay temporarily, but by June these same employees were reduced to working without pay to save the company.

Klotz, in turn, was pouring his personal fortune into the sinking firm. Some distributors, informed that bankruptcy was imminent, salvaged their deposits by taking delivery of incomplete airplanes and trucking them away. Some provided their own engines and flew unupholstered planes with holes in the instrument panel from the factory.

Some rebelled. By midyear, the first lawsuits by creditors were being filed against the Luscombe Airplane Corporation. The final blow was a suit for receivership filed Saturday, June 25, in the 101st District Court against the Luscombe Airplane Corporation. The suit, filed by Maheux Airport, Inc., of Mechanic Falls, ME, claimed that Luscombe was insolvent or in immediate danger of insolvency.

A hearing was held on July 5 on the application for a receiver. The court did indeed find Luscombe insolvent. The court then appointed a trustee, Elijah Crippen, to study the situation and to make a recommendation to the court a month hence.

In a later suit, the IRS alleged that Luscombe Airplane Corporation had not paid taxes, nor had income tax and Social Security withholding been paid, since January 1948. The total asked for in the government suit was $83,194.

While others tried to save the company, a decimated work force continued to work on contracts for Boeing, Consolidated Vultee, and the U.S. Navy, but on a very reduced scale of operation due to the very limited finances of the company. In the Engineering department, Gus Erickson and Merle Mueller worked without pay on the 11C Sedan. Erickson was convinced that the awkward-looking 11A Sedan could be modified inexpensively into a shape that was more aesthetically acceptable to the customer. Klotz gave his nod to the effort.

On July 27, after managing Luscombe's business for nearly a month under the federal court order, Crippen advised Judge William H. Atwell that the firm should continue operating under some reorganization plan. In his report he listed assets at $815,273.03 and liabilities (including undelivered orders and overtime payments) at $692,363.48. Crippen further reported that Luscombe had unfulfilled contracts for about $250,000 with the Navy Air Material Command, Boeing, and Consolidated Vultee, although these contracts were subject to cancellation if the delivery schedules were not maintained. Cash on hand was now less than $10,000! Under the direction of the court trustee, Luscombe officials and auditors were continuing to apply for a Reconstruction Finance loan, while he, the trustee, was trying to find a satisfactory reorganization plan for the company to avoid bankruptcy.

The following month Crippen provided a much more detailed report, listing 10 categories of claimants on Luscombe's assets. The amounts owed ranged from $212,567 in claims secured by contract liens down to $11,526 in checks issued by debtor for insufficient funds.

A hearing was set for August 25 in Judge Atwell's court to determine if Luscombe would be declared bankrupt or allowed to reorganize. He instructed the Federal Referee in Bankruptcy, D.M. Oldham, to set up a meeting of creditors after the firm filed a full list of creditors and assets. At this hearing, Judge Atwell gave Luscombe trustees no more than 30 days to reorganize. Luscombe's attorney, Paul Carrington, pointed out to the judge that both Boeing Aircraft and Texas Engineering and Manufacturing Company (Temco) of Grand Prairie were strong possibilities to take over management of the company.

The Luscombe Company was back in court on October 3 as the referee continued his efforts to settle the company's debts. Referee Oldham reported to the court that Luscombe's priority creditors were owed about $280,000. At this hearing, the creditors were polled and voted in effect to give the bankrupt firm, trustee, and attorneys more time to sell its plant and properties. At this point, Referee Oldham stated: "We might as well tell the stockholders now (essentially meaning Leopold Klotz, who owned nearly 90 percent of the stock) that they won't get anything."

Production at Luscombe now ceased. The postwar Luscombe organization had produced 4732 Model 8s of all versions and 90 Model 11As. Now the factory was silent. The trustee authorized a skeleton staff of about 12 persons to maintain plant security, fill orders for parts, and handle clerical work.

Under the reorganization plan finally adopted, Temco set up a Luscombe holding company that bought all of the stock owned by Klotz. Temco then loaned the holding company $500,000 to settle Luscombe's debts. The plan was approved on January 25 in Judge Atwell's court, contingent upon an affirmative vote by the creditors holding two-thirds of the total Luscombe debt. The final details of Temco's plan to reorganize the bankrupt Luscombe Airplane Corporation were approved by Judge Atwell on February 13, 1950.

During Luscombe's heyday, the factory sign outside the plant proudly announced that the Silvaire was "Built by 1200 Texans." When the company folded, a mere 135 loyal Texans joined the suit for unpaid wages.

After the federal bankruptcy referee stripped Klotz of all interests in the Luscombe Company, and after Temco had purchased his stock at a small portion of its original value, Klotz concluded his personal affairs in Dallas and moved back to New York City.

The Luscombe name had been a proud one in general aviation manufacturing for more than two decades. From the time of Lindbergh's New York-to-Paris flight in 1927, when the Monocoupe first flew, through the Golden Age of Aviation, to the remarkable postwar boom in lightplane manufacture, Luscombe was there.

Now, sadly, Luscombe was history.

Silvaires soldier on

exas Engineering and Manufacturing Company (Temco) officially became the owners of the bankrupt Luscombe Airplane Company on February 13, 1950. H.L. Howard, vice president and general manager of Temco, was approved as president of the reorganized Luscombe Company by Judge Atwell. Howard informed the court that the company would specialize in building a single-engine, crop-spraying airplane. He further stated that the company would also pursue a government contract for several hundred small military liaison airplanes. Temco had been studying this possibility for some time and Luscombe's bid for the government contract would be submitted April 15.

Gus Erickson, Luscombe's former chief engineer, had quit Luscombe and joined Temco in August 1949. Now he returned to the Luscombe factory. When production ceased in October 1949, six nearly completed aircraft remained on the assembly lines: five 8Fs and one T8F sprayer aircraft. Erickson and his small team immediately began to convert the T8F sprayer to the T8F-L configuration to compete for the government contract. He obtained a backup aircraft by repurchasing a 1948 T8F from a former Luscombe distributor. The competition was for the Army Field Forces observation reconnaissance aircraft. Luscombe engineering had originally submitted the T8F-L design proposal for such a plane in August 1948.

The instrument panels were removed and replaced with a new compact flight and engine instrument quick-change subpanel mounted with Dzus fasteners. The team removed the spray tanks from the sprayer, installed landing flaps on the T8F, and equipped both planes with a swing-out engine mount for the new 90-hp Continental injector-type engine. Fuel capacity was increased with the installation of two 17½-gallon tanks.

The USAF conducted the preliminary evaluation for the Army at Wright Field, Dayton, OH. Aeronca and Taylorcraft were eliminated from the competition and the three finalists—Luscombe, Piper, and Cessna—completed the competition, starting May 8, at Fort Bragg, SC. This latter phase consisted primarily of operations under field and simulated combat conditions.

Cessna won the competition. The Cessna entry was not an off-the-shelf airplane; it had been built specifically for the purpose. But the Cessna represented what the Air Force *meant*, rather than what it *said* it wanted. The Cessna entry was based on the Cessna 170 and built around the Continental O-470 190-hp engine. The plane became the L-19 (later, O-1) Bird Dog for which Cessna received an initial order for 400.

Merle Mueller

Project engineer Merle Mueller conducts climb flight test of production T-8F. This model is the only one produced by Temco during a brief production run in 1950.

Without the military contract to sustain volume production, Temco management reassessed the production possibilities for the Luscombe factory. The Sedan and the Crop Master were abandoned. Temco decided to begin using the considerable airframe inventory on hand to build enough of the basic Model 8F to evaluate the strength of the market. In addition, Temco consolidated all aircraft activities by moving the Temco Swift assembly lines to Garland. The Temco-Luscombe entering production in September was essentially an early 1948 Model 8F, equipped with flaps and utilizing bronze trim.

Temco's 8F production was short-lived. Temco obtained substantial subcontracts for the Consolidated Vultee B-36 and subsequently decided to discontinue all personal aircraft construction as of December 31, 1950. In April 1953, the stockholders voted overwhelmingly to merge Luscombe Airplane Corporation into Temco Airplane Corporation (its parent company). With that move, the last vestige of Don Luscombe's dream vanished.

Silvaire Aircraft Company

Temco's tools and equipment for manufacturing Silvaires lay idle for nearly three years. Late in 1953, Temco decided to dispose of the Silvaire Model 8 production rights, tooling, and equipment. Temco called for bids from the aircraft industry and Otis T. Massey of Fort Collins, CO, was among those who responded.

Otis Massey had a long acquaintance with Luscombe. He and his partner, Harry Ransom, had formed the Massey-Ransom Flying Service at Christman Field near Fort Collins, CO, in mid-1937. Massey-Ransom Flying Service had been appointed as a Luscombe dealer in September 1938, only weeks after the Luscombe Model 8 50 had been certified. Otis had taken delivery of a 50

First airplane produced by Silvaire Aircraft Co. (NC 9900C) prior to first flight. Pictured (l. to r.) are: Richard West, Otis Massey, F. Wally Diletto, and Jesse Eggleston.

at the factory that December. At that time Otis placed an order for a Model 4, which he also flew from the factory in January 1939.

Massey's company would eventually produce the very last Silvaire. It is ironic that the Model 4 he purchased in 1939 (serial number 405) would be the last Model 4 ever built. During World War II the Massey-Ransom Flying School swelled to a peak of 55 employees and represented one of the largest payrolls in Fort Collins. When Luscombe started producing lightplanes after the war, Otis Massey again began selling Luscombes. He continued to do so until the company's demise in 1949.

Massey was convinced that the market for two-place airplanes would return, and he decided that he would like to manufacture them when it did. He envisioned building Silvaires, a few at a time, on order from customers direct to the factory. However, the negotiations with the Temco people were quite protracted.

Massey first visited Temco in January 1954, then again in September and October, and finally in January 1955. On January 26, 1955, the papers were finally signed and all rights to the name and title pertaining to the Luscombe Model 8 aircraft were transferred to Otis T. Massey. Otis supervised the inventory and the crating of the purchased equipment and made the shipping arrangements. By early February 1955, all parts and tooling arrived in Fort Collins. Included with the Model 8 tooling were parts and material sufficient to complete approximately four aircraft.

Massey then incorporated. He held interest in mining claims in Wyoming and Utah, so the firm was incorporated as the Silvaire Uranium and Aircraft Company, a Colorado corporation. The incorporation was completed on May 20, 1955. The first stock offering was issued as a penny stock two months later—three million shares at 10 cents a share. Massey leased an office building and a shop at the airport. Then he hired Jesse Eggleston, a key Luscombe employee who had joined that company before the war. Eggleston reported for work in October and for the next four months he and Massey uncrated the shipment from Dallas and organized the factory for production.

During the first six months of 1956, the factory concentrated on building up its inventory of individual Luscombe parts. In July the seven-man production team began building airplanes, completing the first one in early September. Maiden flight of the first Fort Collins Silvaire, N9900C (serial number S1) was conducted on September 10, 1956.

The corporation purchased 10 acres of land near the airport from the Colorado Board of Agriculture and erected a new 14,000-square foot factory, which was completed on December 23, 1956. Six Silvaires were completed in that factory over the next two years. Otis Massey resigned from the

Board of Directors at the beginning of 1958 and in mid-January the name of the corporation was changed to Silvaire Aircraft Company.

Due to the critical cash position of the corporation, the decision was made in June to sell all the uranium interests belonging to Silvaire Aircraft Company; later that summer, the company obtained much-needed additional financing from the Security Credit Corporation. Then the company went "big time." All of Silvaire's aircraft prior to 1959 were built on a direct factory-to-customer basis. Beginning in 1959, a dealer network was established and the distributor was allowed a discount of 20 percent off of the basic airframe and all accessories. In the three prior years, Silvaire had built and sold eight airplanes; in 1959 the company built 63!

Silvaire was selling the 8F for $4950. By comparison, Forney Industries, another Fort Collins lightplane manufacturer, was marketing its competitor, the 90-hp Forney Aircoupe, for $6995.

Silvaire was in the red when their line of credit ran out. The company was unable to obtain any additional capital and the inevitable occurred on May 17, 1960. The last Silvaire rolled out of the factory. Various vendors repossessed equipment during July and August, and Security Credit Corporation began foreclosure procedures late that summer. In January 1961, Security Credit Corporation bid the amount of its loan at a sheriff's foreclosure sale and purchased the Silvaire Aircraft Company. In the five years following its incorporation, Silvaire had built 80 Silvaire Model 8F airplanes.

Larsen Industries

The factory sat idle until 1963, then Security Credit Corporation did as Temco had done before them: they advertised the Luscombe Model 8 tooling and Type Certificate for sale. This time the buyer was Moody Larsen of Larsen Industries, Belleville, MI.

Moody Larsen was also no stranger to Luscombes. As a young man, Moody had obtained his pilot's license in 1939 and had purchased a new Model 8 in 1940. After WWII he took over a flying school and at one time was teaching 50 students in seven Luscombes. He established a flying field near Willow Run while working for Kaiser, eventually began operating there as an FBO, and in 1953 established Larsen Industries. In 1959 he bought a new Silvaire (N9944C) from Otis Massey and in 1963 began the design work to install a 150-hp Lycoming O-320 engine in it.

Moody purchased the Type Certificate, tooling, and parts on hand with the intention of building Model 8s on an assembly line in a well-equipped 120-foot-long hangar he owned. Over the years he had become quite proficient at airplane modifications and he planned to build Model 8s with a range of engines—90-hp, 115-hp, and 150-hp. Later, as events unfolded, he was never able to obtain the million dollars or so worth of financing that the venture required.

Moody trucked the tooling to Belleville, MI, in the late spring of 1964. He established a parts department as well as an engineering department and in January 1965 changed the name of the airplane division to Larsen Luscombe Corporation. He operated the parts department for a full year, but then, finding that he couldn't make it pay, he dismantled it.

Larsen's modification plans went forward. He received an STC on August 4, 1965, covering the installation of a 150-hp Lycoming engine conversion for Model 8E and 8F Luscombes. (More than two decades later, he has completed 16 of them.) He went on to obtain STCs for the installation of three other Lycoming engines in Model 8s: the O-235 (115-hp), the O-290-D (125-hp), and the O-290-D2 (135-hp) Lycoming engines. He also holds an STC for the installation of a popular 35-amp alternator.

In 1968, Moody Larsen began negotiation with a group in Atlanta, GA, that was interested in purchasing the Luscombe tooling and Type Certificate and ultimately producing aircraft in Georgia. The group incorporated as Luscombe Aircraft Corporation, a Georgia corporation, on August 28, 1968. Larsen retained an interest in the venture, and for his contribution received cash, notes, and stock. The production drawings and all related engineering were shipped to Georgia; Larsen retained the tooling in Michigan and waited for completion of the financial arrangements. That never occurred. The business never got off the ground, the venture's spearhead died, and today the status of the Type Certificate for the Luscombe Model 8 (#A-694) is in limbo.

Luscombe Association

"You just can't keep a good man down." This folk saying is wonderfully apt for the Luscombes. The airplanes are classics, tried by time and circumstance. Rare Luscombe Phantoms have been restored by dedicated aficionados and the sole surviving Model 4 is currently being restored in California. Beautifully maintained Model 11A Sedans are scattered around the country, and hundreds of gorgeous Model 8s of every mark and combination dot the skies in the United States and abroad.

The last factory-produced Luscombe was rolled out in 1960. But three decades later, the Luscombe is alive and well. Luscombe-type clubs are a part of the glue that holds the pilots and owners of these delightful airplanes together. There are two thriving Luscombe-type clubs, the Michigan-based Luscombe Association and the California-based Continental Luscombe Association. The Luscombe Association is about a decade older.

The Luscombe Association was founded by Gunther Schmidt, a Luscombe enthusiast from Seattle, in the 1960s. The club was originally operated as one of the type clubs under the auspices of the Antique Airplane Association located in Blakesburg, IA. The baton was soon passed to an eager young member of the Association from Omaha, Jay Armstrong. Then Louis Coghill, a prewar Luscombe employee, entered the picture. Lou Coghill had worked for the Luscombe company for two years, from the spring of 1936 to the spring of 1938. In the late 1960s, Lou was raising sheep near Blakesburg, IA. In his spare time he volunteered at the Antique Airplane Association headquarters there. He energetically promoted the Luscombe

Former Luscombe (West Trenton) employee Louis Coghill, ca. 1945, leans on the rudder of his Curtiss Fledgling. In the 1970s, Coghill was instrumental in getting the Luscombe "Alumni" involved with the Luscombe Association and the Continental Luscombe Association.

Kathy Coghill

club and was an officer for a time. He began actively seeking out former Luscombe employees (the "Alumni"). In 1970, Lou successfully organized the first gathering of Luscombe Alumni at Rockford, IL.

A Nebraska man (name now lost), Dick Lawrence, and Robert Shelton (a math professor at Western Illinois University) followed each other in succession as president. Along the way, the club grew and developed into a separate Luscombe Association. John Bergeson joined the organization during the Shelton presidency and continued as a regular member for several years until 1980. The presidents, then as now, shouldered the obligatory functions of regularly publishing a newsletter and organizing the annual fly-in—both wearing activities. Naturally enough, Bergeson, a fellow college professor, was eventually approached by Shelton, who said: "I'm getting kind of tired of running the Luscombe Association; why don't you run it?" Bergeson decided it was right down his alley and said, "Sure." The Bergesons (John and his wife Alice) have been running the Luscombe Association since 1980.

During the Bergeson's tenure the club has grown from about 275 members to about 1200 members. The Luscombe Association newsletter, published bimonthly, stresses technical information relating to maintenance, restoration, and modification.

Alumni at Columbia, CA, May 1986, with Luscombe buffs Jim Zazas (Luscombe historian, kneeling, l.) and Ron Price (Model 4 owner, kneeling, r.). Group is posed in front of Zazas' 8A in which he has just crossed the continent from Kittyhawk, NC. Alums and wives present at this Continental Luscombe Association fly-in are (l. to r.): Ken Cericola, Howard Jong, Ross Funk, Marion King, Alfred King, Bill Shepard, Winona Burgess, Chuck Burgess, Jerry Coigny, Lucy Coigny, Bee Eisenmann, Marty Eisenmann, and Keith Funk.

Luscombe Association fly-ins

In the 1970s and early '80s the annual fly-in was held at the Antique Aircraft Association field at Blakesburg, IA, over the Fourth of July weekend. But if the weather was too bad to fly, the officers couldn't get out there because it was too far to drive. John Bergeson and the other officers then decided to move the fly-in. At about that time a group of people from Moraine Air Park (just south of Dayton, OH) offered their airport and services to the Luscombe Association. Spearheaded by Ralph E. "Reo" Orndorf, a Luscombe Association member, this group now runs the fly-in each year.

The Luscombe Association runs a low-key, sociable fly-in billed as the annual Luscombe Forum. There are no flying events such as aerobatics or spot landing contests. The fly-in emphasizes the natural camaraderie and the sharing of lore and Luscombe information, and culminates in "the Barbecue." Featured during the weekend are trips to the nearby Air Force Museum, an in-depth technical forum, and a judging contest of the many outstanding Luscombes that participate.

Former Luscombe Company employees (the "Alumni") are held in special esteem. Over the years a host of them have attended one or more of the Luscombe Association fly-ins.

Loren Bump

Luscombes parked at Columbia, CA, May 1984; 107 Luscombes attended this Continental Luscombe Association fly-in.

Bergeson's current fleet

The Bergesons are especially well-qualified to operate a successful Luscombe club. They run the Piper Cub Club as well. Furthermore, they have extensive experience in owning and maintaining vintage aircraft. The Bergesons currently own an IFR-equipped, 1966 Cessna 182, a mint-condition Stearman with a Continental 220-hp engine, a Luscombe 8A with an O-200 engine, and a J-3 Cub, which John is presently rebuilding and modifying.

Continental Luscombe Association

The idea for the Continental Luscombe Association (CLA) was born in the summer of 1975 at the Merced (CA) Antique Air Show. Loren Bump, a veteran volunteer for that airshow, was there with his Luscombe 8A. He observed with dismay that his was the only Luscombe on the field. He further observed three couples wearing yellow jackets with a Piper Cub logo on the back. They had come in three J-3 Cubs and they were all parked together. That gave Loren Bump his inspiration, and he thought to himself: "I'm going to start a Luscombe club." At the time, he was unaware of the existence of the Luscombe Association based in the Midwest.

Loren mulled the idea over for the rest of the summer and that fall went to work on it. In September, Loren approached four fellow Luscombe owners that he knew of in the Modesto area. He persuaded those four to become charter members of the club. Their dues became the first $40 that went into the club treasury. Then Loren ran into Mel Jenkins from Fresno. Jenkins was well-known around the Central Valley for his clown act, for which he always used his Luscombe. Mel volunteered to be the editor of the club newsletter. Loren and his wife, Adele, published the first newsletter using a mimeograph machine borrowed from the local EAA chapter in Modesto. That first newsletter, mailed in the early winter of 1975−76, went to 21 members.

CLA grows

The club was originally named the California Luscombe Association (CLA), so called because Loren figured out only people in California (realistically, just in the Central Valley) would belong to it. Loren was quite surprised when the first member from Los Angeles heard about the club through the grapevine and sent in $10. Then he received a letter from Morris J. Crouch, postmarked Salt Lake City, UT. Crouch wrote: "I would join your organization if it wasn't just restricted to Californians." Loren decided to change the club's name just to enroll a member from Utah, and a wrote him back: "Just for you, I'll change the name to 'Continental' Luscombe Association, if that'll get you to join the club." (By 'Continental' Loren meant Continental United

States, *not* Continental engine.) So Crouch joined the club; he is still a member today.

Birgitte Eben (CLA 254), a Danish woman, became the first woman overseas member in 1978. Her Luscombe (registered as OY-ANE) was judged as the best antique aircraft at the Rotterdam fly-in that year. Today the club has overseas members from all over the world: Argentina, Australia, England, Mexico, New Zealand, and more.

First fly-in

The CLA held its first annual fly-in on Loren's birthday, May 8, 1976, at Red Top Ranch, a small, dirt airstrip with a grassy area by the hangar located about 20 miles west of Merced. Twenty-one airplanes, all Luscombes, showed up, including four or five that flew up from southern California. The club had just acquired a new member, Cecil Taylor, from Boise, ID. He couldn't fly his Luscombe out of Boise because of a storm, but he wanted to attend that first fly-in so badly that he hopped a commercial jet, flew down, and joined the gathering.

Competition flying consisted of flour-bombing, spot-landing, and ribbon-cutting contests for which trophies were given. The latter contest consisted of breaking crepe paper stretched low across the runway without touching the runway with the wheels. When the ribbon was lowered to one foot, no one succeeded.

The fly-in was held inside the open hangar. The members just sat around and talked about Luscombes and made new friends. There was no special

One of the attractions at the Luscombe Association's 1990 fly-in was Jack Dunkle's quarter-scale radio-controlled model (1 1/2-hp Zanoha 6-23 engine) of his Model 8, N 1533K. The kit is marketed by J.M.D. Models, Medina, OH.

seminar. Nor had it occurred to the officers to judge airplanes. The airport restaurant cooked for the club, including the fly-in "banquet," an inexpensive spaghetti dinner. There was no place to stay nearby, so that night everybody camped out by their airplanes.

Columbia '77 and on

Later that year, Loren heard about Columbia airport in the Sierra foothills near Sonora. He flew up there, walked to town for a cup of coffee, and looked the place over. He liked the airport, he liked the area, and he just generally fell in love with the place. The CLA held the 1977 fly-in at Columbia and has returned there every year since.

Club membership and fly-in attendance grew steadily. In 1984 they hit a peak of 107 Luscombes at the fly-in. In the late 1970s, the Luscombe "Alumni" began to attend the CLA's annual fly-in at Columbia.

Luscombe "Alumni" become involved

The Luscombe "Alumni" is the name adopted by those people who once worked for the Luscombe Airplane Company. Loren Bump first learned about the Luscombe Alumni through Louis Coghill. Loren ran into Louis about 1976 or 1977 at the Merced antique fly-in. Coghill sent Bump the names and addresses of people he was still in contact with and Loren then made contact with 20 or so Alums. Eventually, as many as 15 alumni couples attended a single fly-in.

Luscombes live on

The CLA is currently 360 members strong. The club is run from Loren Bump's study. Here, a model of Loren's 8A (built by Howard Jong) is suspended from the ceiling. Named the Howard Jong Museum, the study's walls are full of Luscombe photos that date from the mid-1930s to the present.

Here, as elsewhere, the Luscombe story lives on.

Buying and flying
the Silvaire

The Luscombe Silvaire is today as attractive to the eyes of discerning new pilots as it was to the original owners in the booming post-WWII years. As an older generation of loyal owners reluctantly leaves the sky, a new generation waits to get its hands on the Silvaire's well-worn stick and throttle.

Gar Williams offers some comments to these potential buyers on buying (or maintaining) a Luscombe Model 8. Williams is well-qualified to speak out. He is the principal technical adviser to the Luscombe Association. He is the owner of a restoration/maintenance business (AeroCraft, Naperville, IL) that has delivered 23 major projects in 8½ years and conducts 40 annual inspections yearly. He has been flying Luscombes since 1953 and has owned a Luscombe nearly continuously since 1957.

Quality of inspection

Gar's first concern is the quality of the annual inspection: ''Who did the inspection and how well did he do it?''

It's Gar's experience that because the Luscombe is a ''less expensive'' airplane—the people who own them are often operating on a limited budget—there is a propensity to get ''tailgate annuals.'' A ''tailgate annual'' is one where the IA (Inspector of Aircraft) will do an inexpensive inspection on the airplane. The owner removes the inspection plates from the airplane and the IA brings his pickup truck out and conducts the annual inspection at the tiedown. Then the owner puts his logbooks on the tailgate of the pickup and the IA signs them off.

"Almost invariably," states Williams, "an airplane that is inspected in that manner does not get inspected well at all." Important items that need inspection are likely to be missed.

AD compliance

Once one gets by the question of "who did the inspection and how well did he do it", the next question is how well have the ADs *really* been complied with. All Airworthiness Directives (ADs) were issued for a good reason and all must be *carefully* complied with. In the case of the Luscombes, Gar points out three that are really repetitive. It is all too easy for these inspections to be conducted casually, incompletely, or incompetently. And Gar can tell a story on each one.

AD 48-8-2 inspects for cracking of Cleveland wheels with mechanically operated shoe brakes. **AD 51-10-2** requires a thorough inspection of the control cables. **AD 55-24-1** inspects for corrosion of the carry-through spars. (The AD on the spar inspection does not apply to those airplanes built at Fort Collins, Colorado—serial numbers S1 through S86—on which the spars were anodized at the factory before they were installed.)

AD 48-8-2 on Cleveland wheels requires that the wheels be disassembled and the hubs, the wheels themselves, have to be inspected for cracks every 100 hours. Most of the postwar Luscombes have those wheels on them. Gar had one crack on him that had been "inspected" and the result was a very squirrelly Luscombe. The inspector might say, "Gee, I've never seen a crack, so I'll look at it next year," and he'll just sign it off.

The next AD is **51-10-2**, which requires a thorough inspection of the control cables. In this one, the FAA wants the operator to remove the cables from the airplane to inspect them. The reason for the cracking is that, from an engineering standpoint, the size of the pulleys that these 1/8" cables go around is too small. That size was used simply because it was the size of pulley that fit in the wing.

Some owners have tried to solve that problem of cables getting rusty and cracking by installing stainless cables. This is a mistake, because stainless cables generally are not quite as flexible as galvanized, so they crack *sooner*.

Gar was once responsible for the assembly of 18 Luscombes in England. These Luscombes had mostly been in license. By far the biggest problem that he found in reassembling these airplanes was the condition of the cables. There was hardly an airplane that the team put together on which he didn't have to replace at least one of the eight cables. The rudder cables are almost a straight shot and would not appear to be a problem, but Gar had one break *in his hand*! It was rusty back in the last bay, where it normally can't be seen. It was rusty, Gar bent it, and it broke and that airplane was less than six months out of license!

Finally, with respect to **AD 55-24-1** and other corrosion problems, there is a story that has become part of the Luscombe folklore: One long-time Luscombe owner had his tailcone simply *fall off* while he was taxiing out for takeoff one day. The embarrassed fellow came to a rather sudden halt after dragging the rear half of the airplane along by the rudder cables for a few feet.

ADs must be treated with the utmost respect.

Ground-loop damage

After corrosion, the main target of any inspection should be ground-loop damage. A large percentage of Luscombes have been ground-looped at some time or another, and sometimes alignment damage goes undetected. Look particularly for wrinkles in the fuselage skin just behind the door handles. There's also a good chance the landing gear has been replaced (the gear legs in pre-1949 models are weak and tend to fold up easily), so check that carefully, too. Also look for wrinkled skins around the gear legs and the wing spar attach points.

The so-called "Silflex" gear was introduced early in 1948. It was softer and springier, providing a better ride while taxiing. It also did not collapse as easily in a ground-loop as the earlier Luscombe gear. But that strength could be a problem. When the Silflex gear was severely ground-looped, it sometimes damaged the main fuselage structural members.

Luscombe parts

One might expect the parts situation to be hopeless for an airplane whose manufacturer has been bankrupt for 30 years, but Univair in Aurora, CO, has saved the day for many Luscombe owners. Univair still builds and sells hundreds of different Luscombe parts. Luscombe parts are also available from Wag-Aero in Lyons, WI, and from Moody Larsen in Belleville, MI. Advice on parts and maintenance can be obtained from the two type clubs: the Luscombe Association and the Continental Luscombe Association (see chapter 8).

Accident statistics

There can be a dark side to the ownership of a Luscombe Model 8. This is especially true for low-time pilots who received their training in aircraft equipped with tricycle gear. The National Transportation Safety Board (NTSB) in 1979 released a massive study listing accident rates by aircraft types. The NTSB sorted out accident statistics for 33 different types of aircraft for each year from 1972 through 1976. Using FAA estimates of the number of hours flown by each type every year, the NTSB calculated the rates of total accidents and fatal accidents per 100,000 hours. And the numbers make it very clear: In terms of safety, all aircraft are *not* created equal.

Of the 33 aircraft looked at by the NTSB study, the Luscombe 8 had the worst overall accident rate—dead last. In fact, the Luscombe was the worst by a rather large margin; its total accident rate was 45.7 per 100,000 hours, while the 32nd place Cessna 195 rated 38.5. No other two-seat taildragger had an accident rate above 29. By comparison, the Cessna 150 rated just 10.5—nearly five times safer than the Luscombe.

In terms of fatal accidents only, the Luscombe did slightly better: 30th place out of 33, but still the worst of the comparable postwar two-seaters. This suggests that a large proportion of Luscombe accidents were minor runway accidents and ground-loops that didn't kill anybody.

In specific accident categories, the Luscombe ranked poorly in stall, ground-loop (see table below), and undershoot accidents, and had a terrible rate of midair collision: 0.90 per 100,000 hours, more than *triple* the rate of any other aircraft studied and *10 times higher* than the Cessna 150. This is no doubt partly due to the Luscombe's poor visibility.

Accident Statistics

NTSB accident statistics for the five-year period 1972 – 76 rank the Luscumbe 8 ground-loop rate (per 100,000 hours) with comparable two-seat taildraggers.

Aircraft	Ground-loop Rate	Aircraft	Ground-loop Rate
1. Luscombe 8	13.0	5. Taylorcraft	3.6
2. Cessna 120/140	9.0	6. Globe Swift	3.1
3. Aeronca 7 (Champ, Citabria)	7.5	7. Piper J-3 Cub	2.1
4. Piper Super Cub	3.9		

Ground-loops were mentioned in the preceding paragraph. The Luscombe is notorious for its instability on the ground and a powerful, sensitive rudder control. The inevitable result: ground-loops, the embarrassing, tire-screeching spinouts that occur when a pilot lets his airplane get out of control on the ground. NTSB accident statistics show the Luscombe ranks worst among the two-seat taildraggers in ground-loop accidents, with a rate of 13 per 100,000 flight hours. The Taylorcraft, by contrast, has a rate of 3.5.

One former Luscombe owner reported that he checked the logbooks of more than two dozen Luscombes while shopping for his, and didn't find a single one without ground-loop damage at some time in its history. Luscombe pilots, of course, defend the airplane vociferously, saying that pilots with low time or low time-in-type probably account for the majority of ground-loops.

The Luscombe's "ground-loopitis" is caused by several factors, among them weak, balky heel brakes operated through tiny, nearly inaccessible heel pedals; very stiff gear that promotes bouncing; and a powerful sensitive rudder that often leads to overcontrolling by the pilot. (Because of the rudder sensitivity, a surprising number of Luscombe ground-loops occur on takeoff rather than landing.) Tailwheel type and condition also reportedly can be a big factor. The Luscombe is at its worst on pavement; grass runways are more absorbent and slippery, allowing the airplane to squash and skid rather than dance and swerve.

Ground handling

The Luscombe has a reputation of being "squirrelly." But Luscombes are *not* squirrelly if the landing gear is properly aligned and has correct toe-in. However, an improperly replaced landing gear can result in a *very* squirrelly airplane—and this hair-raising situation Gar Williams has also experienced.

The Luscombe is like any other taildragger in that if you take a Cessna 150 pilot who has not had the experience of reacting quickly to the regular handling required of a taildragger, he might have some trouble handling it. But it won't be squirrelly.

Flight handling

If there's some disagreement about how nasty the Luscombe is on the ground, there's much agreement about how nice it is in the air. Pilots in general praise its flying qualities. Pitch and yaw controls are both light and powerful. By contrast, the ailerons are rather stiff—a combination that takes some getting used to when first encountered. Pilots who like the Luscombe's handling qualities and aerobatic capabilities also brag about the stick control—one of the few to be found in a side-by-side aircraft.

The other side of the coin of agility in the air is that it is an "active" airplane in choppy skies. "It's a tiger in rough air," comments one owner.

On the other hand, it handles delightfully at very high altitudes. Luscombe Association president John Bergeson contrasts his O-200 powered 8A with a Piper Pacer he once owned: "At 12,000 feet my 8A is just as stable as a rock, while at 9000 or 10,000 feet the Pacer began to feel as if you were flying on the head of a pin."

Yet another feature of the Luscombe is its small-field capability. It doesn't float during landing, and it climbs well. Thus, the Model 8 can get out of any field that it can get into.

Aerobatics

Many pilots consider the Luscombe 8 to be an aerobatic airplane. These same pilots are often unaware that the Model 8 is no stronger than other airplanes in the same category (i.e., Taylorcraft). The little Luscombe's special "aerobatic" reputation stems from the publication by Luscombe of the recommended entry speeds for a wide variety of maneuvers—including the Cuban eight, full snap on top of loop, and Immelman. In a December 1947 letter to Gene Norris (Luscombe VP of engineering) from the CAA's Fort Worth region, the CAA stated: "On the basis of the above results, it is considered reasonable to assume that the listed maneuvers can be executed safely, provided the recommended entry speeds are not exceeded." With respect to the specific maneuvers mentioned above, the CAA clearly stated: "These maneuvers are considered to require exceptional skill and a reduction in loading from that used in subject test." The letter went on: "It should be noted that the limit load factors for operations for both the 8A and 8E airplanes are −2.2 to +4.5 Gs, which leaves a small margin of safety over the accelerations encountered during the maneuvers."

Accommodations

Detractors complain—and aficionados admit—that the Luscombe is not built for comfort. It is noisy, cold, and cramped. The airplane's visibility is also deficient. Visibility is adequate over the nose during flight, but rather poor in all other directions. As one owner expressed it: "Side visibility is great for a hunchback. After two years, I developed a definite slump." It is probable that the poor visibility accounts for the Luscombe's terrible rate of midair collisions revealed in the aforementioned NTSB study.

Advice to potential taildragger pilots

Once a Cessna 150 (tricycle gear) pilot with a new private license has acquired a Luscombe Model 8, he faces an important task. He must acquire the additional skills necessary to handle a taildragger with safety and confidence.

No two Luscombe instructor pilots give exactly the same advice, but there is general agreement. First and foremost, locate an instructor who is *skilled* with taildraggers to provide dual instruction. Then, ideally (and this is not always possible), start taxiing and flying from a grass strip before moving to hard-surface runways. Grass is a much more forgiving surface than pavement to the Luscombe's stiff gear and is the safest surface to use when practicing the classic wing-down-into-the-crosswind technique.

Make full-stall landings and *keep* the Luscombe stalled. The pilot of a tricycle-gear airplane gets out of trouble by pushing the wheel forward and nailing the nosewheel to the runway. In marked contrast, the pilot of a taildragger stays out of trouble by making a full-stall landing and keeping the stick full back, holding it in his/her gut. This is equally true while landing in a crosswind with the upwind held low.

Gar Williams has noted one less-talked-about psychological phenomenon that affects transition. Many right-handed pilots—even when they've used a control *wheel* with their left hands—want to hold a control *stick* in their right hand. He observes, however, that handling a stick with the left hand becomes easier with practice in the presence of a competent instructor.

The Luscombe flier must also develop the trait of quick feet. The airplane must be kept moving straight down the runway. Deviations must be dealt with promptly—but with rudder *only*, not brakes.

Finally, concerning the subject of brakes: Use the brakes to run up the engine. Otherwise, don't fool with the brakes. If you *must* brake, do not use both brakes at once; use just one at a time. And, again, keep the stick in your gut. The Luscombe steers very well, even in a strong crosswind, with just rudder control. If it doesn't steer well, there is something wrong with the tailwheel steering mechanism.

In the final analysis, taildraggers are not so fearsome as modern pilots make them out to be. Competent training and careful attention by the pilot to a taildragger's demands are the keys.

Don Luscombe's dream

Don Luscombe bought a Curtiss JN-4 in the mid 1920s so that he could fly for pleasure. The Jenny served him poorly. The JN-4's pilot and passenger sat separately in cold, drafty, open cockpits. The occupants had to suit up in flying togs to go flying. Preflight and postflight chores were onerous. On the ground, the heavy, unwieldy Jenny required walkers at the wingtips to help maneuver. The Jenny did not redeem itself in flight. The climb rate was excruciatingly slow; its 60-mph cruise speed was little better.

Don began to dream of creating an appealing lightplane that was everything that the Jenny was not. He founded a company and created the Monocoupe. Don Luscombe's dream was realized well. He founded a second company that led to the creation of the Model 8 Silvaire. Don Luscombe's dream was fulfilled magnificently.

It is now clear than hundreds of pilots will still be flying Luscombes in the 21st century, living Don Luscombe's dream. The old promotor would have liked that.

Organizations

CONTINENTAL LUSCOMBE ASSOCIATION (CLA)
5736 Esmar Road
Ceres, CA 95307
(209) 537-9934

A type club for Luscombe airplanes. Approximately 360 members. The Continental Luscombe Association is open to anyone wanting to join; you do not have to own a Luscombe or be a licensed pilot to join. Annual dues are $10, U.S.; $12.50 (U.S. Funds), Canada; $15 (bank money order or U.S. cash), foreign. Club publishes bimonthly newsletter, *The Luscombe Courant*. CLA hosts an annual fly-in in May at Columbia Airport, Columbia, CA.

LUSCOMBE ASSOCIATION
6438 W. Millbrook Road
Remus, MI 49340
(517) 561-2393

A type club for Luscombe airplanes. Over 1200 members. The Luscombe Association is open to anyone wanting to join; you do not have to own a Luscombe or be a licensed pilot to join. Annual membership dues are $15, U.S.; $20 (U.S. Funds), Canada; $25 (bank money order or U.S. cash), foreign. Club publishes bimonthly newsletter. Luscombe Association hosts an annual fly-in in June at Moraine Airpark, Dayton, OH.

UNIVAIR AIRCRAFT CORPORATION
2500 Himalaya Road
Aurora, CO 80011
(303) 364-7661

Motto: "All Parts for Some . . . Some Parts for All." Specializes in manufacturing aircraft replacement parts for out-of-production aircraft under a Production Certificate issued to the facility. Univair owns the Type Certificates for the Stinson 108 series and Ercoupe/Forney/Alon/Mooney Cadet aircraft. Production of parts for these two aircraft types accounts for about 25 percent of the company's business.

About the author

Stanley G. Thomas is a retired United Airlines engineer. He has been a private pilot since 1946. He has had two technical papers published by the Society of Automotive Engineers Inc., as well as a history of the homesteading period of his hometown, Nezperce, Idaho. This is his second book in the Flying Classics Series.

Index